*What*

## My Pastor

Scotty,

What an amazing work and labor of love. I commend you on your diligence and desire to be both a student and teacher of God's Revelation. I intend to keep your work as a resource for my future exploration and exegesis of Revelation.

Thank You!

Dr. Brain K Whitney

## My Publisher

I Highly refer and recommend to you this Outstanding work by Mr. Julius Scott as a MUST read and study for all Bible Scholars and researchers. Mr. Scott has completed a verse-by-verse compilation of the book of The Revelation of Jesus Christ that compares favorably with all completed works to date by other authors.

Marvin Forehand, Scholar and Educator

## My Customers

Scotty:

WOW? I have read through chapter six of your Book and am being blessed. I am not a scholar like you and cannot comprehend it all, but it is challenging and such a blessing. Thank you, thank you, thank you!

Peg


Hi Dad, keep up the good work in your bible study! Love you Nancy

Nancy Scott-Biggs


Scotty:

I am really enjoying your book on "Explore Revelations" – WOW!
What a goldmine.
Thank you for sharing with us.
We love you and Isabelle!

Ted

# Explore the Book of Revelation

## Julius M. Scott

Copyright © 2009 by Julius M. Scott

*All rights reserved. No part of this book shall be reproduced or transmitted in any form or by any means, electronic, mechanical, magnetic, photographic including photocopying, recording or by any information storage and retrieval system, without prior written permission of the publisher. No patent liability is assumed with respect to the use of the information contained herein. Although every precaution has been taken in the preparation of this book, the publisher and author assume no responsibility for errors or omissions. Neither is any liability assumed for damages resulting from the use of the information contained herein.*

ISBN 0-7414-5646-X

Published by:

1094 New DeHaven Street, Suite 100
West Conshohocken, PA 19428-2713
Info@buybooksontheweb.com
www.buybooksontheweb.com
Toll-free (877) BUY BOOK
Local Phone (610) 941-9999
Fax (610) 941-9959

Printed in the United States of America

Published November 2009

# Dedication

I dedicate this book to my loving Wife, Isobel C Scott. Your Love, Strength, Stability and Encouragement throughout the years have made this book possible. Explore Revelation has matured because of the numerous hours of your proof reading the early versions of this study.

As I write this book your health is failing and you are residing at the Trinity Nursing Home in Round Rock. I visit you each day and bring treats to the staff of Trinity twice a Month. My unconditional love and support will last forever.

Thank you Isobel,

For your years of loving support!

# Acknowledgments

I want to thank my Wife for her years of dedicated support through the 56 years of our marriage. Isobel your support has been a key factor in the completion of this effort. I thank you and will Love you forever.

I am thankful for the proofreading of the final version of this book by a dear friend of my Wife and me, Minnie Sherman.

I am thankful for the editing of the final version of Explore Revelation by my daughter Nancy Scott-Biggs.

Thank you JOY (Just Older Youth) Sunday school class for your encouragement and comments.

Scripture quotations taken from the HOLY BIBLE, CONTEMPORARY ENGLISH VERSION. Copyright 1995, American Bible Society

The American Bible Society is glad to grant authors and publishers the right to use up to one thousand (1,000) verses from the Contemporary English Version text in church, religious and other publications without the need to seek and receive written permission.

Scripture quotations taken from the HOLY BIBLE, NEW INTERNATIONAL VERSION. Copyright 1973, 1978, 1984 by International Bible Society. Used by permission of Zondervan Publishing House.

The NIV text may be quoted in any form (written, visual, electronic or audio) up to and inclusive of one thousand (1,000) verses without express written permission of the publisher, provided the verses quoted do not amount to a complete book of the Bible nor do the verses quoted account for 50% or more of the total text of the work in which they are quoted.

# Preface

The Bible is filled with prophecy particularly in the Old Testament. Most do not give accurate time periods of the predicted occurrence but most imply prompt results. When Joseph interpreted Pharaoh's dream he sent into motion a fourteen year long event. These two seven year events saved many lives but enslaved all the people in the Nation of Egypt to Pharaoh (See Genesis 41).

Daniel's interpretation of Nebuchadnezzar's dream covered a much longer period of time. Approximately 1,100 years. The kingdoms involved are tabulated below. The dates are all approximations.

| Part | Material | Empire | Period of Domination |
|------|----------|--------|----------------------|
| Head | Gold | Babylonian | 606 B.C. - 539 B.C. |
| Chest | Silver | Medo-Persian | 539 B.C. - 331 B.C. |
| Belly | Bronze | Grecian | 331 B.C. - 146 B.C. |
| Legs | Iron & Clay | Roman | 146 B.C. - A.D. 476 |

The Revelation of Christ, as given to John, covers the time period from Christ's Birth to the end of the earth as we know it.

I have found much conflicting opinions in what is being taught about Revelation. I have prepared for you all the best of what I have learned about Revelation. My desire is that you receive as much joy from our loving God, as presented in Revelation, as I have.

# About the Author

Julius M (Scotty) Scott is a retired Electronics Engineer. I worked for Sperry Gyroscope Company for 17 years. Sperry was a defense contractor and nearly everything was classified. In 1969 I joined Ford Aerospace at the Johnson Manned Space Center in Houston. I was with Ford Aerospace for 21 years. Most projects at Ford Aerospace were public domain and open to the public. One of my projects there was the Color Scan Converter. The first Video back from the Moon the Broadcast Industry accepted and converted it to broadcast quality video. The Broadcast Industry found the Video had so many problems that they demanded NASA provide broadcast standard video or they would not broadcast NASA's video. I was the lead Engineer on the project that provided the equipment that converted the space video to Broadcast Standard Video. At Ford Aerospace I did not go to work I went to play. My best days were spent chasing electrons around a printed circuit board.

Since retirement I have been fascinated with the book of Revelation. I have attended every Revelation class that has been presented in my vicinity for the past 15 years. I have led the study of Revelation in two different churches.

I have found much conflicting opinions in what is being taught about Revelation. I have prepared for you all the best of what I have learned about Revelation. My desire is that you receive as much joy from our loving God, as presented in Revelation, as I have.

# Explore Revelation

## Index

| Title | Chapter | Page |
|---|---|---|
| Dedication | i | 1 |
| Acknowledgements | i | 2 |
| Preface | i | 3 |
| About the Author | i | 4 |
| Index | i | 5-7 |
| **Introduction** | **i** | **8-9** |
| Housekeeping | 1 | 10 |
| **Chapter 1** | **1** | **10-25** |
| Blessing | 1 | 10-12 |
| Seven Churches | 1 | 13 |
| Trinity | 1 | 14 |
| Jesus Return | 1 | 15-17 |
| Matthew 24:30-31 | 1 | 17 |
| Alpha and Omega | 1 | 19-20 |
| John's Witness | 1 | 21 |
| Christ and Churches | 1 | 22 |
| **Chapter 2** | **2** | **26-44** |
| Ephesus | 2 | 26-32 |
| Smyrna | 2 | 32-35 |
| Pergamum | 2 | 35-38 |
| Thyatira | 2 | 38-44 |
| **Chapter 3** | **3** | **45-55** |
| Sardis | 3 | 45-47 |
| Philadelphia | 3 | 47-51 |
| Laodicea | 3 | 51-55 |
| **Chapter 4** | **4** | **56-60** |
| Throne of God | 4 | 56-60 |
| **Chapter 5** | **5** | **61-65** |
| Scroll | 5 | 61-65 |
| **Chapter 6** | **6** | **66-71** |
| White Horse | 6 | 66 |

5

| | | |
|---|---|---|
| Fiery Red Horse | 6 | 67 |
| Black Horse | 6 | 67 |
| Pale Green Horse | 6 | 67 |
| Fifth Seal | 6 | 69 |
| Sixth Seal | 6 | 70 |
| **Chapter 7** | **7** | **72-78** |
| Four Angels | 7 | 72-73 |
| Saints | 7 | 74-78 |
| **Chapter 8** | **8** | **79-83** |
| Seventh Seal | 8 | 79-81 |
| First Trumpet | 8 | 80 |
| Second Trumpet | 8 | 80-81 |
| Third Trumpet | 8 | 81 |
| Fourth Trumpet | 8 | 81-82 |
| Eagle | 8 | 82-83 |
| **Chapter 9** | **9** | **84-89** |
| Fifth Trumpet | 9 | 84-87 |
| Sixth Trumpet | 9 | 87-89 |
| **Chapter 10** | **10** | **90-92** |
| Little Scroll | 10 | 91-92 |
| **Chapter 11** | **11** | **93-99** |
| Two Witnesses | 11 | 93-96 |
| Seventh Trumpet | 11 | 97-98 |
| Destroy the Earth | 11 | 98 |
| **Chapter 12** | **12** | **100-109** |
| Review | 12 | 100-102 |
| Birth of Christ | 12 | 102-104 |
| War in Heaven | 12 | 105-109 |
| **Chapter 13** | **13** | **110-115** |
| Satan's Team | 13 | 110-113 |
| **Chapter 14** | **14** | **116-123** |
| 144,000 | 14 | 116-117 |
| Fall of Babylon | 14 | 118 |
| Mark of Beast | 14 | 119-120 |
| Harvest of Believers | 14 | 120-123 |

| Chapter 15 | 15 | 124-126 |
|---|---|---|
| Preparation for Bowl | 15 | 124-125 |
| Chapter 16 | 16 | 127-133 |
| Review | 16 | 127-128 |
| First Bowl | 16 | 129 |
| Second Bowl | 16 | 129 |
| Third Bowl | 16 | 129 |
| Fourth Bowl | 16 | 129-130 |
| Fifth Bowl | 16 | 130 |
| Sixth Bowl | 16 | 130 |
| Seventh Bowl | 16 | 132-133 |
| Chapter 17 | 17 | 134-138 |
| Great Prostitute | 17 | 134-138 |
| Chapter 18 | 18 | 139-144 |
| Angel | 18 | 139-142 |
| Rejoice | 18 | 143-144 |
| Chapter 19 | 19 | 145-150 |
| Hallelujah | 19 | 145-146 |
| Wedding | 19 | 147-148 |
| White Horse | 19 | 147-150 |
| Chapter 20 | 20 | 151-154 |
| 1000 years | 20 | 151-153 |
| Rule with Jesus | 20 | 152 |
| Satan's Release | 20 | 152-153 |
| Judgment | 20 | 153-154 |
| Chapter 21 | 21 | 155-163 |
| New Earth | 21 | 155-156 |
| New Heaven | 21 | 156 |
| Holy City | 21 | 158-163 |
| 12,000 Stadia | 21 | 159 |
| Wall | 21 | 160-161 |
| Temple | 21 | 162-163 |
| Chapter 22 | 22 | 164-170 |
| River of Life | 22 | 164-168 |
| Warning | 22 | 169-171 |
| Summary | i | 171-191 |

# Introduction to the study of Revelation

The Revelation of Christ, as given to John, covers the time period from around the birth of Jesus Christ to the end of the earth as we know it.

John relates the situation that led to the writing of this Revelation in (1:1-20). John tries to describe the majesty of the risen Jesus Christ and His relationship with the Churches. Jesus gives special instructions to the seven churches of Asia Minor and to the Universal Church of today in (2:1-3:22).

John sees a vision of God Almighty on his throne. All of Christ's believers and the heavenly angels are worshiping God (4:1-11). The qualifications of Jesus Christ to open the seals are given without mentioning such things as the creation of the universe. Christ's death on the cross and his resurrection are so important to mankind that Christ's other qualifications were not even mentioned. God gives a scroll with seven seals to the Lamb, Jesus Christ (5:1-14). Jesus starts to open the seals one by one. As each seal is opened a new event takes place. These judgments, although severe, are partial judgments and are limited to part of the Earth.

Four riders on horses appear as the first seals are opened. They represent war, famine, disease, and death (6:1-8). When the fifth seal is opened John sees those killed for their belief in Christ gathered before the throne of God (6:9-11). These that were killed for their testimony will rule the nations with Christ during the 1000 year period that Satan is bound in the bottomless pit.

When the sixth seal is opened there is a huge earthquake, stars fall from the sky, and the sky rolls up like a scroll. What could cause such things to happen to the earth? Could this disturbance to the earth, be man's first attempt to destroy the earth (6:12-17)? With the advent of the Atomic age man now has the ability to destroy the Earth. Another vision displays a huge multitude before the throne of God; they worship God and Jesus (7:1-17). Do you see yourself in this multitude?

When the seventh seal is opened (8:1-5) another series of God's limited judgments are announced by seven angels with seven trumpets. These trumpet judgments are also limited judgments. One third of the earth is subject to these judgments. The seventh trumpet judgment introduces the seven bowl judgments. The bowl judgments are total judgments and involve the entire earth.

Revelation ends with a message of warning and hope for men and women of every generation. Christ is victorious! All evil has been destroyed. Marvel at God's grace with believers and his power over evil, and remember the hope of this victory for all believers.

# A little housekeeping before we start.

I use two fonts throughout this study. My comments are in Times New Roman black type. The Bible Study text is in *Lucida Handwriting black print.* The Biblical reference text is in **Times New Roman black bold print**. Therefore the black regular print is merely opinions of the writer and is not to be confused with the infallible word of God as presented in the Bible. The **Times New Roman Black Bold** text is directly from the NIV version of the Bible. The first six chapters of bible text come from the Contemporary English Version (CEV) of the Holy Bible. Chapters 7 through 22 have bible text from the New International Version (NIV) of the Holy Bible. Neither of these two versions of the bible will allow anyone to use more than 1000 verses or a complete book of the bible. To remain within these copyright requirements I have selected to use the CEV for the first six chapters and the NIV for the remainder of Revelation. There remains some controversy about the infallibility of the Word of God (Bible). My experience has taught me that when we have trouble believing the Bible it is an indication we need further study of this marvelous book.

## REVELATION CHAPTER 1

John recorded a vision he received from Christ for the seven churches in Asia and for Churches throughout history. This book promises a blessing for those who read and do what it commands.

*1 This is what God showed to Jesus Christ, so that he could tell his servants what must happen soon. Christ then sent his angel with the message to his servant John. 2 And John told everything that he had seen about God's message and about what Jesus Christ had said and done. (CEV)*

John, the Author of Revelation, was the only one of Jesus' original disciples who was not killed for the faith. John also wrote the Gospel of John and the letters 1, 2, and 3 John. John was in exile on the island of Patmos in the Aegean Sea when he wrote Revelation. John was sent to Patmos by the Romans because of his witness about Jesus Christ.

Revelation is a book about the present and the future. Revelation proclaims Christ's final victory over evil and the reality of eternal life with God and His Christ. It offers hope to all believers, especially those who have suffered for their belief. Revelation teaches us about Jesus Christ and how we should live for him now. We learn that (1) Jesus Christ is coming again, (2) evil will be judged, and (3) the dead will be raised to judgment, resulting in eternal life or destruction.

God (the Father) gave his plan to Jesus Christ (the Son), who revealed it to John. Revelation shows Christ's identity and God's plan for the end of our world as it is today. It focuses on Jesus Christ, his second coming, his victory over evil, and the establishment of his kingdom.

As you read and study Revelation don't focus so much on the timetable of the events or the details of John's imagery that you miss the main message – the infinite love, power, and justice of the Lord Jesus Christ.

Revelation is uncovered, unveiled or revealed in style. This style of ancient literature usually featured spectacular and mysterious imagery. Most of such literature was written under the name of an ancient hero. John had studied Jewish works, but this book is different in several ways: (1) John uses his own name rather than the name of an ancient hero, (2) John denounces evil and leads people to high Christian standards, (3) and John offers hope rather than gloom. John was not attempting to predict the future; he was a prophet of God describing what God had shown him.

Jesus allowed John to see and record certain future events so they could be an encouragement to all believers. The visions include many signs and symbols that explain what is to happen. What John saw was indescribable, so he used illustrations to show what it was like. When reading this symbolic language, we don't have to understand every detail. Realize that John's imagery shows us that Christ is indeed the glorious and victorious King of Kings and Lord of Lords.

*3 God will bless everyone who reads this prophecy to others, and he will bless everyone who hears and obeys it. The time is almost here. (CEV)*

Revelation reveals the future. These events are spectacular, but you have nothing to fear if you are on God's side. When you consider the future have confidence because Christ has already saved you. Revelation foretells future events. Revelation teaches about who God is and what he will do for us. The prophecies are important principles about God's character and promises. If you study Revelation you will get to know God better and learn to trust him completely.

Typical news reports today are filled with violence, scandal, and political haggling. News reports are depressing and make you wonder what will happen next. God's plan for the future provides inspiration and encouragement. You know God will intervene in history to conquer evil. John encourages churches to read this book aloud so everyone can hear it and take it to heart. Be assured of the fact that God will triumph.

When John says "the time is near," it is hard for us to reconcile that with the fact he wrote that nearly 2000 years ago. John is urging his readers to be ready at all times for the Last Judgment and the establishment of God's kingdom. We will hear of many people claiming they know when the end is near. Jesus told us that only the Father knows when the end of the earth, as we know it, will be. There are many events that you can watch for that will be revealed in the study of Revelation.

*4 From John to the seven churches in Asia. I pray that you will be blessed with kindness and peace from God, who is and was and is coming. May you receive kindness and peace from the seven spirits before the throne of God. 5 May kindness and peace be yours from Jesus Christ, the faithful witness. Jesus was the first to conquer death and he is the ruler of all earthly kings. Christ loves us, and by his blood he set us free from our sins. 6 He lets us rule as kings and serve God his Father as priests. To him be glory and power forever and ever! Amen. (CEV)*

Jesus told John to write to seven churches that know and trust John and had read his earlier letters. The letters were addressed so that they could be read and passed on; following the main Roman road clockwise around the province of Asia (now called Turkey).

The "seven spirits" is another name for the Holy Spirit. The number seven is used throughout Revelation to symbolize completeness and perfection. (John 3:6 and Acts 1:5)

**John 3:6 Flesh gives birth to flesh, but the Spirit gives birth to spirit. (NIV)**

**Acts 1:5 For John baptized with water, but in a few days you will be baptized with the Holy Spirit." (NIV)**

The Trinity – the Father ("him who is, and who was, and who is to come"), the Holy Spirit ("the seven spirits"), and the Son (Jesus Christ) – is the source of all truth. (John 14:6, 17; 1 John 2:27) Thus we can be assured that John's message is reliable and is God's word to us.

**John 14:6 Jesus answered, "I am the way and the truth and the life. No one comes to the Father except through me. (NIV)**

What are we talking about here? Is this a ticket to an exclusive group? No! Heavens No! It means we cannot accomplish acceptance by God without the redeeming blood of Jesus Christ to cover our sins. Due to the sinful nature of mankind we are incapable of living the sinless life. God recognized our sinful nature and sent us His sinless Son, Jesus Christ, to be the sin offering for the sins of the World. Rejoice in your acceptance, the only cost is your belief!

**John 14:17 The world cannot accept him, because it neither sees him nor knows him. But you know him, for he lives with you and will be in you. (NIV)**

We are given insight into what resources are within each believer. God lives with you and will be in you because his Holy Spirit is within you. Wow, you have God dwelling within you, how does that make you feel? As God's thoughts were spoken and the Universe came into existence, how powerful then are your thoughts? Do YOUR THOUGHTS

CREATE YOUR LIFE? What a powerful concept! However; there is a catch. As we look at Jesus' life we see a repetitive requirement to his healing and miracles. How many times do you remember Jesus asking the intended recipient of a healing if they believe? You must believe to receive! If you don't believe your thoughts you might as well not have them. You must believe to receive.

**I John 2:27 As for you, the anointing you received from him remains in you, and you do not need anyone to teach you. But as his anointing teaches you about all things and as that anointing is real, not counterfeit--just as it has taught you, remain in him. (NIV)**

What is John saying here? Is he saying we are an island and do not need anyone to guide and advise us? No that is not what John is saying! The bible is written so that anyone can understand it if they are earnest about their study of the bible. That does not mean a one time reader can understand the bible; no but, if you become diligent about the study of the bible you will reach an understanding that is sufficient for you. Is John telling us that all we need is within us now? Does the anointing teach us all we need to know about living a meaningful Christian life? The bible's sixty-six books are complementary, in that the understanding of one book makes it easier to understand other books of the bible. It takes all sixty-six books to understand the bible.

Others, besides Jesus Christ, have risen from the dead. Lazarus was raised from the dead by Jesus yet he later died again. The people who the prophets and apostles raised from the dead later died. Jesus was the first who rose from the death in an imperishable body (1 Corinthians 15:20), never to die again. He is the firstborn from the dead.

**1 Corinthians 15:20 But Christ has indeed been raised from the dead, the first fruits of those who have fallen asleep. (NIV)**

Do you hesitate to witness about your faith in Christ? Do you feel the change in your life has not been spectacular enough? But you do qualify as a witness for Jesus! Not because of what you did for Jesus; but because of what Jesus has done for you. Christ's love was demonstrated by setting us free from our sins by his blood. Jesus guarantied you a place in his kingdom! Jesus made you a priest to administer God's love to others. The fact that the all-powerful God has offered eternal life to you is nothing short of spectacular. The gift of eternal life with God and His Christ is almost too good to believe.

Jesus is your all-powerful King, victorious in battle, glorious in peace. Jesus is not a humble teacher; he is the only Son of God. When you read John's description of the events, remember they are truths from the King of Kings. Do not read his words for their interesting and amazing portrayal. Let the truth about Jesus control your life, increase your faith in Jesus, and strengthen your commitment to follow him.

*7 Look, he is coming with the clouds. Everyone will see him, even the ones who struck a sword through him. All people on earth will weep because of him. Yes, it will happen! Amen. (CEV)*

Jesus is returning to earth (see also Matthew 24). Jesus' second coming will be visible and victorious. All people will see him arrive (Mark 13:26), and they will know it is Jesus. When Jesus comes he will conquer evil and judge all people according to their beliefs and deeds.

**Matthew 24:2 "Do you see all these things?" he asked. "I tell you the truth, not one stone here will be left on another; every one will be thrown down." (NIV)**

Herod the Great began to remodel and rebuild the temple, which had stood for nearly 500 years, around 35 BC. Herod made the temple one of the most beautiful buildings in Jerusalem – not to honor God, but to appease the Jews whom he ruled. This rebuilding/remodeling was completed around 64 AD. The Romans completely destroyed the temple and the entire city of Jerusalem in 70 AD. Is this what Matthew is bringing to light in Matthew 24:1- 2?

**Matthew 24:22 If those days had not been cut short, no one would survive, but for the sake of the elect those days will be shortened. (NIV)**

**Matthew 24:29 "Immediately after the distress of those days 'the sun will be darkened, and the moon will not give its light; the stars will fall from the sky, and the heavenly bodies will be shaken.' 30 "At that time the sign of the Son of Man will appear in the sky, and all the nations of the earth will mourn. They will see the Son of Man coming on the clouds of the sky, with power and great glory. 31 And he will send his angels with a loud trumpet call, and they will gather his elect from the four winds, from one end of the heavens to the other. (NIV)**

Wow, we covered a lot of ground there. There is something left out at the end of Revelation Chapter 6 that is covered here.

At the end of Revelation Chapter 6 we see the earth in great distress. Does Matthew 24: 30-31 explain what happened? Revelation Chapter 7 starts out like nothing happened. This intervention by Jesus Christ is needed to fill the gap between Revelation Chapter 6 and 7.

Matthew states and restates that the event that happens at the end of Revelation Chapter 6 cannot be predicted and only God, the Father, knows when it will happen. However it does state that we must be aware of the conditions that could precipitate the nuclear disaster that seems to happen at the end of Revelation Chapter 6.

We see here that the dead will be raised first and then the believers that are still alive will meet with the Lord in the air. Some say the dead are in a better place but here we are told the dead are still on earth and are in a sleep like state. They will be the first raised when Jesus Christ returns.

**Mark 13:26 "At that time men will see the Son of Man coming in clouds with great power and glory. (NIV)**

Christ's arrival in the clouds with great power and glory will be seen through the world by all. Is Mark confirming what Matthew said in Matthew 24:30 &31?

We see here the clear description of two books one is the Book of Life which reflects our choice. If you accept Jesus Christ as your personal Lord and Savior then you are in the Book of Life. The significance of the Book of Life is your acceptance into the New Jerusalem and dwelling with God for eternity. The other book; however is usually not the one we consider. The other book is a record of your deeds, good and bad, which we will be individually judged by. All your deep dark secrets will be exposed for all to see; however you will have Jesus as your defense, Jesus is the only one that has already paid for your sins.

"Those who pierced him" could refer to the Roman soldiers who pierced Jesus' side as he hung on the cross or to the Jews who were responsible for his death. John saw Jesus' death with his own eyes, and he never forgot the horror of it (John 19:34, 35). My view is that each of us personally pierced Jesus by our commitment of sins. Jesus Christ gave his life for our sins. The penalty for sin is death. Remember in Genesis where the people tried to climb the mountain where Moses was to get a view of God? They were struck dead; sin cannot exist in the presence of God. Therefore; we must have the blood of Christ to remove the stain of sin before we can be in the presence of God. If we were not sinners there would be no need for the death of our sinless Lord and Savior Jesus Christ. The Roman soldiers and the Jewish leadership are no guiltier of taking Jesus' life than each of us.

**John 19:34 Instead, one of the soldiers pierced Jesus' side with a spear, bringing a sudden flow of blood and water. 35 The man who saw it has given testimony, and his testimony is true. He knows that he tells the truth, and he testifies so that you also may believe. (NIV)**

The Jewish holy days were coming and the Jewish leaders did not want a Jew to be hanging on the cross during the holy days. They ask Roman Soldiers to break the legs of the people crucified to hurry along their death. When they came to Jesus he was already dead so they did not break his legs, however they did stick a spear in his side to make sure he was dead.

*8 The Lord God says "I am the Alpha and the Omega, the one who is and was and is coming. I am God All-Powerful!" (CEV)*

The first and last letters of the Greek alphabet are Alpha and Omega. Our God is the beginning and the end of everything. God (the Father) is the Ruler of the past, present, and the future (4:8; Isaiah 44:6; 48:12-15). Without God you have nothing that is forever, nothing that can save your life, nothing that can save you from your sin. Is the Lord your reason for living? Is God the Alpha and the Omega of your life? Honor God who is the beginning and the end of all existence, wisdom, and power. Please use all the love, wisdom, truth, justice and kindness that exist within you.

**Revelation 4:8 Each of the four living creatures had six wings and was covered with eyes all around, even under**

**his wings. Day and night they never stop saying: "Holy, holy, holy is the Lord God Almighty, who was, and is, and is to come." (NIV)**

Is this instruction as to how we should spend our day? Are your days crowded with things that must be done? Do you make it a point to make Jesus a part of each decision you make every day?

**Isaiah 44:6 "This is what the LORD says-- Israel's King and Redeemer, the LORD Almighty: I am the first and I am the last; apart from me there is no God. (NIV)**

Although we do not see a lot of people worshiping man made gods in our neighborhood, what about the worship of material things. Has God's abundant supply of things in our life caused us to believe these possessions are purely our own accomplishment? Do you remember to thank God for all the things you have in your life today?

Isaiah is attempting to correct the worship of man made gods and drive home the fact that there is only one true God!

*9 I am John, a follower together with all of you. We suffer because Jesus is our King, but he gives us the strength to endure. I was sent to Patmos Island, because I had preached God's message and had told about Jesus. (CEV)*

Patmos is a small rocky island in the Aegean Sea, about 50 miles offshore from the city of Ephesus on the Asia Minor (now Turkey) seacoast.

The Christian church was facing severe persecution by the Roman Empire. Almost all believers were socially, politically, or economically suffering because of this Roman

Empire-wide persecution. Some Christians were even being killed for their faith. John was exiled to Patmos because he refused to stop witnessing about the life of Jesus. We may not face persecution for our faith as the early Christians did, but even with our freedom few of us have the courage to share God's Word with others. If we hesitate to share our faith during easy times, how will we do during times of persecution?

*10 On the Lord's day the Spirit took control of me, and behind me I heard a loud voice that sounded like a trumpet. 11 The voice said, "Write in a book what you see. Then send it to the seven churches in Ephesus, Smyrna, Pergamum, Thyatira, Sardis, Philadelphia, and Laodicea." 12 When I turned to see who was speaking to me, I saw seven gold lampstands. 13 There with the lampstands was someone who seemed to be the Son of Man. He was wearing a robe that reached down to his feet, and a gold cloth was wrapped around his chest. 14 His head and his hair were white as wool or snow, and his eyes looked like flames of fire. (CEV)*

Can you imagine John's situation here where he is attempting to describe the indescribable? Some say this is the Scriptural proof of the distinction by the Apostles between Jewish worship on the Sabbath, Saturday and the Christian worship on the Lords Day, Sunday. Sunday was chosen by the Apostles because it is the day of Christ's Resurrection.

The seven lamp stands are the seven churches in Asia, and Jesus stands among them. Jesus protects the churches with his love and reassuring power. Jesus Christ is still among the churches today, through his Spirit. When a church faces persecution does it remember Christ's deep love and compassion? All Churches should remember Christ's concern for purity and his intolerance of sin when it is experiencing internal strife and conflict.

Jesus is about to tell us what's wrong with the seven Asian churches and what's wrong with the churches of today. Jesus also tells what is good about the seven Asian churches and what is good and in need of encouragement in the churches of today.

Jesus is this man "like a son of man." Jesus the Messiah has the title of Son of Man many times in the New Testament. John recognized Jesus because he lived with him for three years. John had been with Jesus in Galilee and recognized Him as the glorified Son of God at the transfiguration (Matthew 17:1-8). Jesus appears as the Almighty Son of Man. His hair indicates his wisdom and divine nature. His blazing eyes symbolize judgment of all evil. The golden sash reveals Jesus to be the high priest who goes into God's presence to obtain forgiveness for our sin.

Jesus had been praying for the cup (crucifixion of Christ) to be avoided if possible, but that God's will be done. Here we see the options available. Moses died and was buried, but his body never saw corruption because an angel contended with Satan for his body. Elijah on the other hand was taken by God from the earth.

*15 His feet were glowing like bronze being heated in a furnace, and his voice sounded like the roar of a waterfall. 16 He held seven stars in his right hand, and a sharp double-edged sword was coming from his mouth. His face was shining as bright as the sun or moon. (CEV)*

John's description of the risen Christ is limited by John's ability to comprehend what is occurring around him. The task of describing the indescribable is something we will only understand when we meet Christ.

The power and force of his message is represented by the sword in Jesus' mouth. His words of judgment are as sharp as swords (Hebrews 4:12). Again, in Revelation, the power of the word is brought into focus. Why do we not utilize this power for ourselves? We have been told God resides within us, yet we are so timid as to not even consider our dreams as things that should and could become our reality. Why not let our thoughts create our lives?

**Hebrews 4:12 For the word of God is living and active. Sharper than any double-edged sword, it penetrates even to dividing soul and spirit, joints and marrow; it judges the thoughts and attitudes of the heart. (NIV)**

The power of the spoken work is emphasized here. How careful are you about what you speak? Do you use the power of verbal command to design your life? Do you verbalize your desires? Can a dream come true if you have no dream?

*17 When I saw him, I fell at his feet like a dead person. But he put his right hand on me and said: "Don't be afraid. I am the first, the last, 18 and the living one. I died, but now I am alive forevermore, and I have the keys to death and the world of the dead. (CEV)*

John wondered if the church could survive and stand against the oppression as the Roman Empire stepped up its persecution of Christians. But Jesus reassured John that he and his fellow believers had access to God's strength to face these trials. If you are facing difficult problems, remember that the power available to John and the early church is also available to you (1 John 4:4).

**I John 4:4 You, dear children, are from God and have overcome them, because the one who is in you is greater than the one who is in the world. (NIV)**

Our sins have convicted us and sentenced us to death. Jesus holds the keys of death and Hades. Jesus Christ alone can free us from eternal bondage to Satan. Jesus has the power and authority to set us free from sin's control. Because Jesus Christ holds the keys to both Hades and Death, believers do not have to fear death. All we must do is turn from sin and turn to him in faith. When we attempt, without Jesus, to control our lives we set a course that leads directly to hell. But when we place our lives in Christ's hands, He restores us now and resurrects us later to an eternal, peaceful relationship with him. Again God's presence within us is stated. If God is with us who can prevail against us? Remember God spoke the Universe into existence, what are you doing with the power within you? Do you believe YOUR THOUGHTS CREATE YOUR LIFE? Why not verbalize those thoughts and command your future to be whatever you desire.

*19 Write what you have seen and what is and what will happen after these things. 20 I will explain the mystery of the seven stars that you saw at my right side and the seven golden lampstands. The seven stars are the angels of the seven churches, and the lampstands are the seven churches. (CEV)*

Who are the "angels of the seven churches"? Some say that they are elders or pastors of the local churches. Because the seven letters in chapter 2 and 3 contain reprimands, it is doubtful that these angels are heavenly messengers. If these are earthly leaders or messengers, they are accountable to God for the churches they represent. The Pastorship of any Church is an awesome responsibility.

If you have questions, suggestions, comments or criticisms please send me an e-mail at scotty80@juno.com.

Julius M (Scotty) Scott
A Student of Revelation

# REVELATION CHAPTER 2

## The Letter of Ephesus

*1 This is what you must write to the angel of the church in Ephesus: I am the one who holds the seven stars in my right hand, and I walk among the seven gold lampstands. Listen to what I say. (CEV)*

As we proceed through the letters to the churches we will establish a large variety of names for Jesus Christ. When we see these names anywhere in the bible we know them to be referring to our Lord and Savior, Jesus Christ.

The one who walks among the seven churches is Jesus. He holds the messenger of the churches in his right hand. Jesus has power and authority over all churches and their leaders. Ephesus had become a large church, and Jesus' message would remind them that He alone is the head of the body of believers. "To the angel" refers to the pastors/leaders of the church in Ephesus.

Ephesus was the capital of Asia Minor. It was a center of land and sea trade. The Jewish population of Ephesus was large; only second to Alexandria. Ephesus was one of the most influential cities in the eastern part of the Roman Empire. The temple to Artemis (Diana) was located in this city. Artemis was a major industry in the manufacture of images of this goddess (Acts 19:21-41).

Paul taught in Ephesus for three years and warned the Ephesians that false teachers would come and try to draw people away from the faith (Acts 20:29-31). False teachers did indeed cause problems in the Ephesian church, but the church resisted them, as we can see from Paul's letter to them (Ephesians). The Ephesian culture was very sex oriented. Paul spent much of his ministry in this city and knew that they had resisted false teaching. The Ephesian church became the third most important Christian city after Jerusalem and Antioch.

Demetrius and his fellow craftsmen would continue to hound the church at Ephesus in an attempt to protect their occupations and livelihood. The Ephesus church was able to withstand this attack and remain faithful to Christ. Is your church capable of resisting the cultural normal activities surrounding them and still remain faithful to Christ and his teachings?

Most churches have strong leaders that the entire congregation tends to accept and follow. These people are prime targets of Satan and when he can convert or misdirect one of them it is a major victory for Satan and much damage can be done to that church.

*2 I know everything you have done, including your hard work and how you have endured. I know you won't put up with anyone who is evil. When some people pretended to be apostles, you tested them and found out that they were liars. (CEV)*

Does God care about your church? If you are tempted to doubt it, look more closely at these seven letters. The Lord of the universe knows each of these churches and its precise situation. In each letter, Jesus told John to write specific people, places, and events. He praised believers for their successes and told them how to correct their failures. Just as Jesus cared for each of these churches, he cares for yours. He wants it to reach its greatest potential. The group of believers with whom you worship and serve is God's vehicle for changing the world. Take it seriously, God does.

Over a long period of time, the church in Ephesus had steadfastly refused to tolerate sin among its members. This was not easy in a city noted for immoral sexual practices associated with worship of the goddess Artemis. We also are living in times of widespread sin and sexual immorality. It is popular to be open-minded toward many types of sin, calling them personal choices or alternative life-styles. But when the body of believers begins to tolerate sin in the church, it is lowering the standards and compromising the church's witness. Remember that God's approval is infinitely more important than the world's.

*3 You have endured and gone through hard times because of me, and you have not given up. (CEV)*

Christ commended the church at Ephesus for:

1 Working hard,
2 Persevering,
3 Resisting sin,
4 Critically examining the claims of false apostles, and
5 Enduring hardships without becoming weary.

Every church should have these characteristics. But these good efforts should spring from our love of Jesus Christ. Both Jesus and John stressed love for one another as an authentic proof of the gospel (John 13:34; 1 John 3:18, 19). In the battle to maintain sound teaching and moral and doctrinal purity, it is possible to lose a charitable spirit. Prolonged conflict can weaken or destroy our patience and affection. In defending the faith, guard against any structure or rigidity that weakens love.

**John 13:34 "A new command I give you: Love one another. As I have loved you, so you must love one another. (NIV)**

Can we rise above our petty doubts and jealousness to reach a love for each other as Christ loved each of us? Can we remember that the annoying individual, that just cut you off in traffic, is created in the image of God just as you are? Can you set aside our pre judgment of individuals and focus on the good characteristics of that individual instead of the thing that annoy us?

**I John 3:18 Dear children, let us not love with words or tongue but with actions and in truth. 19 This then is how we know that we belong to the truth, and how we set our hearts at rest in his presence. (NIV)**

As Christ developed his twelve disciples to carry on his work after his departure he traveled around the country doing good deeds wherever he traveled. Christ demonstrated his love by what he did. When favors were needed Christ granted them without demanding something in return. Christ's only requirement was a matter of faith. Is your Faith strong enough to get you what you want? Do we all need to work on our faith daily?

*4 But I do have something against you! And it is this: You don't have as much love as you used to. 5 Think about where you have fallen from and then turn back and do as you did at first. If you don't turn back, I will come and take away your lampstand. (CEV)*

John had once commended the church at Ephesus for its love of God and others (Ephesians 1:15), but many of the church founders had died, and many of the second-generation believers had lost their zeal for God. They were a busy church, the members did much to benefit themselves and the community, but they were acting out of the wrong motives.

Work for God must be motivated by love for God or it will not last. Many of our churches today have reached or exceeded the 80% occupancy rule. When an organization reaches its 80% occupancy rule, the tendency is the put off growth until the finances are clear. The ever increasing demand for organization funds makes the growth process even harder. The fact is one cannot have improvement without change. All change is not improvement; however, improvement can only come with change.

John records the things the church at Ephesus must correct:

1 You have forsaken your first love,
2 Remember the height from which you have fallen,
3 Repent and do the things you did at first.

New believers rejoice at their newfound forgiveness. But when we lose sight of the seriousness of sin, we begin to lose the thrill of our forgiveness (2 Peter 1:9). In the first steps of your Christian life, you may have had enthusiasm without knowledge. Do you now have knowledge without enthusiasm? Both are necessary if we are to keep love for God intense and untarnished (Hebrews 10:32, 35). Do you love God with the same fervor as when you were a new Christian?

**2 Peter 1:9 But if anyone does not have them, he is nearsighted and blind, and has forgotten that he has been cleansed from his past sins. (NIV)**

Paul is talking about faith, goodness, knowledge, self control, perseverance, godliness, brotherly kindness, and love which will keep you from being ineffective and unproductive.

For Jesus to "remove your lamp stand from its place" would mean the church would cease to be an effective church. Just as the seven-branched candlestick in the temple gave light for the priests to see, the churches were to give light to their surrounding communities. But Jesus warned them that their lights could go out. In fact, Jesus himself would extinguish any light that did not fulfill its purpose. The church had to repent of its sins.

*6 But there is one thing you are doing right. You hate what the Nicolaitans are doing, and so do I. (CEV)*

The Nicolaitans were believers who compromised their faith in order to enjoy some of the sinful practices of Ephesian society. The name Nicolaitans is held by some to be roughly the Greek equivalent of the Hebrew word for "Balaamites." Balaam was a prophet who induced the Israelite to carry out their lustful desires (2:14; Numbers 31:16). When we want to take part in an activity that we know is wrong, we may make excuses to justify our behavior, saying that it isn't as bad as it seems or that it won't hurt our faith. Christ has strong words for those who look for excuses to sin. When you are disobedient to local speed limit laws do you consider it a sin?

When Balaam could not curse the Israelites as they moved into the Promised Land, even after being offered great rewards, he taught Balak how to corrupt them with the use of sexual favors.

**Numbers 31:16 "They were the ones who followed Balaam's advice and were the means of turning the Israelites away from the LORD in what happened at Peor, so that a plague struck the LORD's people. (NIV)**

Though John, Jesus commended the church at Ephesus for hating the wicked practices of the Nicolaitans. Note that they didn't hate the people, just their sinful actions. We should accept and love all people and refuse to tolerate all evil. God cannot tolerate sin, and he expects us to stand against it. The world needs Christians who will stand for God's truth and point toward right living.

*7 If you have ears, listen to what the Spirit says to the churches. I will let everyone who wins the victory eat from the life-giving tree in God's wonderful garden. (CEV)*

To overcome is to be victorious by believing in Christ, persevering, remaining faithful, and living as one who follows Christ. Such a life brings great rewards (21:7).

Two trees were in the Garden of Eden – the tree of life and the tree of the knowledge of good and evil (Genesis 2:9). Eating from the tree of life brought eternal life with God; eating from the tree of knowledge brought realization of good and evil. When Adam and Eve ate from the tree of knowledge, they disobeyed God's command. So they were excluded from Eden and barred from eating from the tree of life. Eventually, evil will be destroyed and believers will be brought into a restored paradise. In the New Jerusalem, everyone will eat from the tree of life and will live forever.

**Genesis 2:9 And the LORD God made all kinds of trees grow out of the ground-- trees that were pleasing to the eye and good for food. In the middle of the garden were the tree of life and the tree of the knowledge of good and evil. (NIV)**

## The Letter to Smyrna

*8 This is what you must write to the angel of the church in Smyrna: I am the first and the last. I died, but now I am alive! Listen to what I say. (CEV)*

The city of Smyrna was about 30 miles north of Ephesus. It was nicknamed "Port of Asia" because it had an excellent harbor on the Aegean Sea. The church in this city struggled against two hostile forces: a Jewish population strongly opposed to Christianity, and a non-Jewish population that was loyal to Rome and supported Emperor Worship. Persecution and suffering were unavoidable in an environment like this.

*9 I know how much you suffer and how poor you are, but you are rich. I also know the cruel things being said about you by people who claim to be God's people. But they are really not God's people. They are a group that belongs to Satan. 10 Don't worry about what you will suffer. The devil will throw some of you into jail, and you will be tested and made to suffer for ten days. But if you are faithful until you die, I will reward you with a glorious life. 11 If you have ears, listen to what the Spirit says to the churches. Whoever wins the victory will not be hurt by the second death. (CEV)*

Persecution comes from Satan, not from God. Satan, the devil, will cause believers to be thrown into prison and even killed. But believers need not fear death, because it will only result in their receiving the crown of life. Satan may harm their earthly bodies, but he can do them no spiritual harm. The "Synagogue of Satan" means that these Jews were serving Satan's purpose, not God's, when they gathered to worship. "Ten days" means that although persecution would be intense, it would be relatively short. It would have a definite beginning and end, and God would remain in complete control.

Pain is part of life, but it is never easy to suffer, no matter what the cause. Jesus commended the church of Smyrna for its faith in suffering. He then encouraged the believers that they need not fear the future if they remained faithful. If you are experiencing difficult times, don't let them turn you away from God. Instead let them draw you toward greater faithfulness. When we are born we have physical life but are spiritually dead. When we accept Christ as our Lord and savior we gain spiritual life. When a believer dies the spiritual life continues. If we persevere in the faith we will not lose our spiritual life even when we lose our physical life. Trust God and remember your heavenly reward (22:12-14).

Smyrna was famous for its athletic Games. A crown was the victory wreath, the trophy for the champion at the games. If we have been faithful, we will receive the prize of victory, eternal life (James 1:12). The message to the Smyrna church was to remain faithful during their suffering because God is in control and his promises are reliable. Jesus never says that by being faithful to him we will avoid troubles, suffering, and persecution. Rather, we must be faithful to him in our suffering. Only then will our faith prove to be genuine. We remain faithful by keeping our eyes on Christ and on what he promises us now and in the future (Philippians 3:13, 14; 2 Timothy 4:8).

Believers and nonbelievers will both experience physical death. All people will be resurrected, but believers will be resurrected to eternal life with God while nonbelievers will be resurrected to be punished with a second death, eternal separation from God (20:14; 21:8; 22:15).

Most of these are obvious but how about those who practice magic arts? Does that include the Horoscope, Fortune tellers, Palm readers, and such? The Old Testament tells us what happens when you use such information sources.

## The Letter to Pergamum

*12 This is what you must write to the angel of the church in Pergamum: I am the one who has the sharp double-edged sword! Listen to what I say. (CEV)*

The city of Pergamum was built on a hill. The hill created a natural fortress about 1,000 feet above the surrounding countryside. Pergamum was a center of Greek culture and education. It was a sophisticated city with a very large library. It was the center of four cults. The city's chief god was Asclepius, who was considered the god of healing. Its symbol was a serpent much like the medical symbols of today. People came to Pergamum from all over the world to seek healing from this god.

Jesus' sharp, double-edged sword represents the power of God's Word. God's Word will be used to strike dead the nonbelievers in future chapter of Revelation. It is the ultimate authority and true judge. It will be used to separate believers from nonbelievers. You must believe and accept Jesus Christ as your Lord and Savor to receive the eternal rewards of living in God's New Jerusalem.

*13 I know that you live where Satan has his throne. But you have kept true to my name. Right where Satan lives, my faithful witness Antipas was taken from you and put to death. Even then you did not give up your faith in me. 14 I do have a few things against you. Some of you follow the teaching of Balaam. Long ago he told Balak to teach the people of Israel to eat food that had been offered to idols and to be immoral. 15 Now some of you are following the teaching of the Nicolaitans. (CEV)*

Satan had four idolatrous cults (Zeus, Dionysus, Asclepius and Athena) in Pergamum. Christ called it the city "where Satan has his throne." Not only was the city dominated with satanic cults, there was a large group that worshiped the Roman emperor as a god. The church at Pergamum held fast to their faith even as one of their members was martyred. Can your church remain faithful as our surrounding society becomes more and more tolerant about what activities are considered normal?

Believers in Pergamum experienced great pressure to compromise or leave the faith. Do you experience the same tug of Satan to draw you into immoral activities? Antipas did not compromise; will the future be able to say the same about you? Antipas was faithful and he died for his faith. Some churches today tolerate teachings or practices what Christ opposed. Compromise can be defined as consent reached by mutual concessions. Cooperate with people as much as you can. Be careful to avoid any participation that could lead to immoral practices. Remember to love one another.

Is there room for differences of opinion among Christians in some areas? How about the differences between denominations? Do most still believe in Jesus Christ as our Lord and Savior? Do most stick to the basic truths of the Bible? Must we always be on guard against heresy and immoral activities? Do not bow to pressure to be tolerant of activities that deny your faith.

When the Israelites were entering the Promised Land it caused great concern by the existing residence. How would you feel about a half million men camping outside your town? King Balak offered a king's ransom to Balaam if he would place a curse on the Israelites (Numbers 22:1-41). Balaam refused at first but after the offer of three huge rewards Balaam taught Balak how to draw the youth of Israel into sexual immoral activities (Numbers 31:16; 2 Peter 2:15; Jude 1:11). The eating of food sacrificed to false gods and sexual misconduct caused a plague to strike the Israel nation. The resulting plague started killing off the Israelites and did not stop until the guilty party's family were stoned to death. Where three offers of a king's ransom were unsuccessful, sexual misconduct succeeded. The church today must guard against people that would lead people away from God.

*16 Turn back! If you don't, I will come quickly and fight against these people. And my words will cut like a sword. (CEV)*

This sword is God's judgment against rebellious nations (19:15, 21) and all forms of sin.

God's vengeance is swift and exact, notice the vengeance was accomplished through the word of Christ. Have you ever recognized a sin that you have been committing and told God you were sorry, ask for forgiveness, thanked god for the forgiveness and expressed your love for God. Have you given your voice the opportunity to command the outcome you desire?

*17 If you have ears, listen to what the Spirit says to the churches. To everyone who wins the victory, I will give some of the hidden food. I will also give each one a white stone with a new name written on it. No one will know that name except the one who is given the stone. (CEV)*

During the 40 years the Israelites traveled in the desert, God provided manna from heaven for their physical nourishment (Exodus 16:13-18). Jesus as the bread of life (John 6:51) provides spiritual supplementation and purification that separates us from our sinful ways.

It is unclear, to me, what the white stones are or exactly what the names on each will be. Because they relate to the hidden manna, they may be symbols of the believer's eternal nourishment, or eternal life. The stones are significant because each will bear the new name of every person who truly believes in Christ. They are the evidence that a person has been accepted by God and declared worthy to receive eternal life. A person's name represented his or her character. God will give us new names and new hearts.

## The Letter to Thyatira

*18 This is what you must write to the angel of the church in Thyatira: I am the Son of God! My eyes are like flames of fire, and my feet are like bronze. Listen to what I say. 19 I know everything about you, including your love, your faith, your service and how you have endured. I know that you are doing more now than you have ever done before. (CEV)*

Do you believe your church is large enough? Christ praised the church in Thyatira for their growing good deeds. Does that mean we should increase our church outreach? Should the size of the church control its ability to help others? Can we grow in good deeds and remain the same size in the long term? Must we grow in love, faith and acts of service? Is Christ suggesting here that we grow in membership and services? Are Membership and Services tied together in the long term? A church that is not growing in membership is soon in financial trouble just to maintain existing services. For a church to have continual growth in its services/outreach it must have continual growth in its revenue base.

*20 But I still have something against you because of that woman Jezebel. She calls herself a prophet, and you let her teach and mislead my servants to do immoral things and to eat food offered to idols. (CEV)*

Is this really Jezebel or just a name that indicates the character of the person involved? Either way teaching that sin is permissible is a road to destruction. We all sin and we will never completely overcome that; but, we must always be on guard to repent from the sins as we become aware of them. Jezebel was considered the most evil woman who ever lived (1 Kings 19:1, 2; 21; 2 Kings 9:7-10; 2 Kings 30-37). All churches should be diligent to guard against teachings that lead people away from Christ as our Lord and Savior.

Sexual immorality is prevalent in our society today. With a divorce rate around 50% how much of that was caused by infidelity? Of divorces caused by abuse, how much of that was caused by sexual immorality in the beginning. Do you consider sexual immorality serious? Have you heard the saying "If you lay down with a dog and you get up with flees?" Have you noticed that people that have been married for a long time take on each others sayings or mannerisms? When a man uses the services of a prostitute he gets up with whatever STD she may have but also part of her personality. It work both ways, the prostitute gains part of the customers personality. My understanding is that man and wife become one in the long term. After 56 years together my wife and I tend to agree on most things. There are exceptions but they are rare. Sex outside of marriage always hurts someone. It violates the commitment necessary for lasting relationship.

Sexual immorality has tremendous power to destroy families, churches, and communities because it destroys the integrity on which these relationships are built. God wants to protect us from hurting ourselves and others; thus we are to have no part in sexual immorality, even if our culture accepts it.

Idol worship often involved meat sacrifices that were burnt. Eating this meat was not wrong in its self; however, it could be offensive to new believers that were not well grounded in Christian beliefs. If any of your actions cause a fellow believers to stray from their Christian beliefs or weakens their faith you should refrain from that activity. The fact that you know there is only one God does not mean that everyone understands the uniqueness of God.

*21 I gave her a chance to turn from her sins, but she did not want to stop doing these immoral things. (CEV)*

To repent means to stop doing the sinful activities you are doing. However, sin is often habit forming. Once a pleasure is tasted it is often repeated until it becomes a habit. Habits are not stopped they are changed. That is to change a habit one must substitute a different activity in place of the old habit. The first step is to acknowledge the sin and recognize what a hold it has on your life. Once you acknowledge sin you must find some acceptable activity to replace the sin with. A habit is not formed overnight and is not easily corrected. Some say it takes 30 continuous days to break a habit. I am sure there is something to do with the intensity of desire in the time period it takes to change any activity.

*22 I am going to strike down Jezebel. Everyone who does these immoral things with her will also be punished, if they don't stop. 23 I will even kill her followers. Then all the churches will see that I know everyone's thoughts and feelings. I will treat each of you as you deserve. (CEV)*

Do you believe you will eventually be judged by Jesus Christ? Christ judgments will be on all your deeds, nothing will be left out. Even with all our faults Christ still loves us. Can you imagine loving someone that is as disobedient as we are? God's feelings for us must be similar to our feelings about our children. Those darling little angels grow up to teenagers; but, they do survive to become, in most cases, responsible adults. We need to confess those "hidden sins" and ask Christ to help us overcome them.

*24 Some of you in Thyatira don't follow Jezebel's teaching. You don't know anything about what her followers call the "deep secrets of Satan." So I won't burden you down with any other commands. 25 But until I come, you must hold firmly to the teaching you have. (CEV)*

How do you accomplish deeper spiritual life? Is it through serious bible study? What does serious bible study mean to you? Can you go to a bible study class and let someone else lead you through the lesson? Must you read the bible and all reference material to gain better understanding of the subject you are studying? Is this a skill you can farm out and let someone else do the hard work? Are you led by whatever the teacher tells you, or do you search out your own truth for yourself? Some people are gifted and can absorb complex concepts easily; however, most people only gain knowledge by personal sustained effort. There are no "deep secrets" or "guaranteed" short-cuts to greater spirituality.

*26 I will give power over the nations to everyone who wins the victory and keeps on obeying me until the end. (CEV)*

As we see the believers gathered into the New Jerusalem and the evil ones tossed into the lake of burning sulfur, what is left to rule over? There must be a huge group of good people that have not confessed their belief in Christ remaining. However we see where all those that are not in the Book of Life are thrown into the lake of burning sulfur. Are the people that are in the Book of Life given a selection as to where they want to live in the New Jerusalem or not? Are these the people that believers will rule over? Christ promises that those that overcome will reign with him over the nations. (Psalm 2:8, 9; Isaiah 30:14; Jeremiah 19:11; 1 Corinthians 6:2, 3; Revelation 12:5; 19:15; 20:3, 4).

**Psalms 2:8 Ask of me, and I will make the nations your inheritance, the ends of the earth your possession. 9 You will rule them with an iron scepter; you will dash them to pieces like pottery." (NIV)**

Is this again saying, ask and you will receive?

Christ's rule over the Nations will be complete and unrelenting. Our rule over the Nations will by Christ's infallible commands.

42

Are you ready to judge the world? How about your own household? How about your own life? Are you using the Law of Attraction to rule your own life? If not, why not?

We will see later in Revelation that as Christ was born Satan was waiting to capture and destroy him.

The power of the word is stated over and over! Why not use that power now? Have you verbalized your desires and dreams? We see demonstrations of the power of words every day, in Sermons, Seminars, TV Broadcast, Radio and others. Why not use some of that power to fulfill your fondest dreams?

This is the imprisonment of Satan for 1000 years. He will not be around to tempt everyone so how do we know who truly believes and who does not truly believe. Satan must be released again for a short period to test the beliefs of those that claim to accept Christ's offer of everlasting life with God.

*27-28 I will give each of them the same power that my Father has given me. They will rule the nations with an iron rod and smash those nations to pieces like clay pots. I will also give them the morning star. (CEV)*

Christ is called the morning star in 2:28, 22:16 and 2 Peter 1:19. A morning star appears just before dawn, when the night is coldest and darkest. When the world is at its bleakest point, Christ will burst on the scene, exposing evil with his light of truth and bringing his promised reward.

Christ is giving us assurance that Revelation is from Him and not the imagination of John.

**2 Peter 1:19 And we have the word of the prophets made more certain, and you will do well to pay attention to it, as to a light shining in a dark place, until the day dawns and the morning star rises in your hearts. (NIV)**

The nature of light is stated again here. Light can penetrate the darkness but darkness cannot penetrate the light. Your righteous light cannot be darkened by the sin all around you; but you do have the ability to bring a sinner to Christ.

*29 If you have ears, listen to what the Spirit says to the churches. (CEV)*

Let us hear and obey the message of Revelation concerning the Church now and forever.

# Revelation Chapter 3

## The Letter to Sardis

*1 This is what you must write to the angel of the church in Sardis: I have the seven spirits of God and the seven stars. Listen to what I say. I know what you are doing. Everyone may think you are alive, but you are dead. (CEV)*

The original city of Sardis was built on a hilltop. As the city grew they ran out of space on the hilltop and started building on the valley below. Sardis grew into a very affluent city with much of the distraction we have today. Have you experienced the feeling that there are always more things to do than there is time to do them?

As noted before the Seven Spirits refer to the Holy Spirit of God, and the seven stars are the leaders of the churches.

The church in Sardis, although not a small church, is like most small churches of today. In general they are struggling to maintain the existing facilities and support their pastoral organization. People attend church to receive whatever is missing in their spiritual life. When that need is not fulfilled they reduce or withdraw their financial support and attendance from the church. The church in Sardis was spiritually dead. Sardis like most cities today had many sinful elements and were in need of a spiritual rebirth.

We live in a time and place that allows us to be involved is so many things that we have no time for family or friends. Our children are involved in so many sports or special interest activities that we spend most of our time driving them to and from these activities. Many moms feel like they are a chauffeur service for their children. If there is any quiet time in our lives we cram something else into that time slot. This leaves us in danger of being like the church at Sardis. How are you keeping Christ in your life?

*2 Wake up! You have only a little strength left, and it is almost gone. So try to become stronger. I have found that you are not completely obeying God. 3 Remember the teaching that you were given and that you heard. Hold firmly to it and turn from your sins. If you don't wake up, I will come when you least expect it, just as a thief does. (CEV)*

The church at Sardis was in need of revival, they needed to return to the activities they did when the church was new. As the church ages the original worshipers do not completely instill their belief into the younger members. As this practice continues the spiritual belief become watered down until it is easily corrupted. We see this demonstrated over and over in the Old Testament, where one generation does not adequately teach the next generation about spiritual things. Thank God for the exception to that general practice.

Spiritual growth requires continuous growth in the knowledge of the Lord through study of God's Word. This study brings us back to the basic of our faith. It is important to increase our understanding of the Lord through careful study. We must never abandon the basic truths about Jesus. His sacrifice for our sins is permanent! He will always be the Son Of God! Never accept any new truth that contradicts Biblical teachings.

*4 A few of you in Sardis have not dirtied your clothes with sin. You will walk with me in white clothes, because you are worthy. 5 Everyone who wins the victory will wear white clothes. Their names will not be erased from the book of life, and I will tell my Father and his angels that they are my followers. (CEV)*

When you accept Jesus Christ as your personal savior your name is entered into the Book of Life. Jesus Christ promised he would not lose one of those given to him by the father. You not only have assurance of being in the Book of Life but you also have a guarantee that you will not be lost. Being "dressed in white" proves you have been set aside for God and made pure. The book of life registers you as belonging to God. If you are in the book of life you will be introduced to the host of heaven as belonging to Jesus Christ.

*6 If you have ears, listen to what the Spirit says to the churches. (CEV)*

Does this sound like a Father urging his child to follow his instructions? Just because a church is large and prosperous does not mean it is a good church. One of the Churches functions is to bring the nonbeliever to Christ and help the nonbeliever understand and accept Christ as their Lord and Savior.

## The Letter to Philadelphia

*7 This is what you must write to the angel of the church in Philadelphia: I am the one who is holy and true, and I have the keys that belonged to David. When I open a door, no one can close it. And when I close a door, no one can open it. Listen to what I say. (CEV)*

Philadelphia was kind of a frontier town. It was built in a frontier area between the well developed coastal region and the plains of central Asia Minor (Now Turkey). This community kept barbarians out of the coastal region and brought Greek culture and language to the area. The citizens of Pergamum founded the community of Philadelphia. An earthquake destroyed the city in AD17. The after shocks caused most people to reside outside of the city limits. The key of David symbolizes Jesus' authority to invite people into the future kingdom. Jesus Christ's judgment is certain what he opens no one can shut, and what he shuts no one can open.

*8 I know everything you have done. And I have placed before you an open door that no one can close. You were not very strong, but you obeyed my message and did not deny that you are my followers. 9 Now you will see what I will do with those people who belong to Satan's group. They claim to be God's people, but they are liars. I will make them come and kneel down at your feet. Then they will know that I love you. 10 You obeyed my message and endured. So I will protect you from the time of testing that everyone in all the world must go through. (CEV)*

Again Christ's knowledge of all churches is repeated. How does that make you feel about where you are worshiping? Are you confident you are in the right place? Here again we have an open invitation to join Christ, through the open door, and have our names written in the Book of Life. Entry into the book of life again is only through Jesus Christ.

There are many beliefs about the "hour of trial," none of which have a wide acceptance. Christ has promised that Satan cannot harm your spirit even though your physical body may receive damage. Remember when this was written was a period of great persecution for members of the Christian belief. All we have to worry about is patient, persistent following of Christ's teaching. Does the 'hour of trial' mean that your belief in Christ as your Lord and Savior will be tested to determine if you really believe? Has your faith been tested? Does testing strengthen our beliefs?

*11 I am coming soon. So hold firmly to what you have, and no one will take away the crown that you will be given as your reward. (CEV)*

Have you ever used the expression "we are the same age" in reference to you and your associates maturity? Does that include your spiritual gifts, talents and experiences? We are all individuals with some similarities to other people but yet unique. Why would God make us that way? If two people agree on everything then only one is thinking and the other is just going along with the leader. We are different so that when we come together we can strengthen each other. If we were all the same there would be no need or advantage of community. We are expected to hold on to our spiritual gifts, talents, experiences and yes even our knowledge gained from the community we associate with. God expects us to use all our resources for Him. Philadelphians were commended for their effort to obey, and instructed to hold on to what strength they had. If you feel your spiritual strength lacking, use what you have anyway. With use, your spiritual strength will grow stronger. As you study God's Word (Bible) and associate with other Christians your faith will strengthen and your knowledge will grow.

*12 Everyone who wins the victory will be made into a pillar in the temple of my God, and they will stay there forever. I will write on each of them the name of my God and the name of his city. It is the New Jerusalem that my God will send down from heaven. I will also write on them my own new name. (CEV)*

The New Jerusalem is the future home for all those in the Book of Life. We will look closer at this New Jerusalem later in this study. For now accept that it will far exceed anything we can experience on this earth. We may have lost a precious tradition of doing business based on the handshake between two people. At one time a name was all you needed to be assured that a task/job/project would be accomplished in a professional and honest way. Today there are too many Lawyers in the way of each person accepting personal responsibility for all we do and say. The new name given by God will consider your whole being.

**Rev 21:2 I saw the Holy City, the new Jerusalem, coming down out of heaven from God, prepared as a bride beautifully dressed for her husband. (NIV)**

*13 If you have ears, listen to what the Spirit says to the churches. (CEV)*

Does this again sound like a Father urging his child to follow his instructions? Your growth in spiritual awareness should be a lifetime effort. What we don't use; we lose. If you don't keep up your study of Christ and His teaching you will drift away from His leadership and return to your own desires.

## The Letter to Laodicea

*This is what you must write to the angel of the church in Laodicea: I am the one called Amen! I am the faithful and true witness and the source of God's creation. Listen to what I say. 15 I know everything you have done, and you are not cold or hot. I wish you were either one or the other. (CEV)*

Laodicea was located near a hot springs. An aqueduct was used to bring the hot water to the city; but, by the time it got to Laodicea it was only slightly warm. The water was not cool enough for a refreshing drink or warm enough for a nice hot bath.

The church there had similar characteristics. The worshipers were neither excited nor sharing in their spiritual activities. When we are new in our relationship with Christ we are excited and anxious to share our news with others, as we mature in our faith we become less excited and more comfortable in our faith. We need both knowledge and excitement to do our task of bringing the work of God to all. Much like our community Laodicea was the wealthiest of the seven cities. Laodicea had a thriving banking, manufacturing, and medical industry. This wealth distracted the people from the pursuit of spiritual activities and consumed much of their time in pursuit of material things. Does that sound like all of us today? Should we let Christ fire up our faith and get back into action?

*16 But since you are lukewarm, and neither cold nor hot, I will spit you out of my mouth. 17 You claim to be rich and successful and to have everything you need. But you don't know how bad off you are. You are pitiful, poor, blind, and naked. (CEV)*

Even today some believers assume large material possessions are a sign of God's spiritual blessings. Of course there are those that believe that if you have money you are not to be trusted. Neither of which is true. The church at Laodicea was wealthy and did not find itself struggling to meet current expenses. Sometimes it takes a struggle to get a church to become active in its spiritual tasks.

Some say if we provide the spiritual needs of the congregation the finances will take care of them self. We must recognize that what we can see and buy are less valuable than what is unseen and eternal. The affluence of today can cause us to feel confident, satisfied and complacent. No matter how wealthy you are you have nothing if you do not have a right relationship with Christ. How does your current level of wealth affect your spiritual desire? Instead of centering your life primarily on comfort and luxury, find your true riches in Christ.

*18 Buy your gold from me. It has been refined in a fire, and it will make you rich. Buy white clothes from me. Wear them and you can cover up your shameful nakedness. Buy medicine for your eyes, so that you will be able to see. (CEV)*

Christ tells the Laodicean to buy gold (real spiritual treasures) from him. In this cloth dyeing center Christ tells them to buy white clothes from him (his rightness). Laodicea was the world center for eye salve but Christ told them to get treatment from him to heal their eyes so they could see the truth (John 9:39). Christ was showing the Laodicean that true value was not in material possessions, but in a right relationship with God. Their possessions and achievements were of no value compared to the everlasting future of Christ's kingdom.

Is Jesus speaking directly to us? Does our new economy consume all our energy and leave us too weak to pursue our religious responsibilities? What have you done lately to build your spiritual treasures? What have you done lately to strengthen your righteousness? What have you done lately to improve your recognition of the truth? Does that mean we should spend more time in Bible study and good deeds? Christ went around the country doing good deeds; does that mean we should do the same?

**John 9:39 Jesus said, "For judgment I have come into this world, so that the blind will see and those who see will become blind." (NIV)**

*19 I correct and punish everyone I love. So make up your minds to turn away from your sins. (CEV)*

God will discipline any church that is indifferent to the teachings of Jesus. God's discipline is not meant to punish but to bring people back to a proper relationship with Jesus Christ. Has your passion for Christ weakened as time passes? Have you let your busy life slide into an uncaring attitude? Do you believe the study of God's Word, confession, service and worship can bring you back to a right relationship with God? Just as love can bring the romance back into a marriage, the Holy Spirit can bring you back to a right relationship with Christ.

*20 Listen! I am standing and knocking at your door. If you hear my voice and open the door, I will come in and we will eat together. (CEV)*

In this time when we insist on instant gratification do we lose sight of God's offer of everlasting satisfaction? Do you sometime find yourself feeling indifferent in church or bible study? If you do then you have started shutting God out of your life, be careful. The pleasures of the world only last a few years and then we must face eternity. Jesus is knocking on the door of your heart every time we sense we should turn to him. Jesus wants to have fellowship with us, and he wants us to open up to him. He is patient and persistent in trying to get through to us, not breaking and entering, but knocking. He allows us to decide whether or not to open our lives to him. Do you intentionally keep his life-changing presence and power on the other side of the door? How many times have you pushed Christ out of your mind because you had too many other things to do? If we do not respond to his call now we may not have another chance. If we wait until we have time it may leave us trapped in a situation that requires our life.

*21 Everyone who wins the victory will sit with me on my throne, just as I won the victory and sat with my Father on his throne. 22 If you have ears, listen to what the Spirit says to the churches. (CEV)*

The end of each letter to the churches ends in a plea for the church to pay attention and take to heart what is written to the church. Although they were written 2000 years ago they are still relevant to each of our churches today. Which letter speaks most directly to your church? Which has the greatest bearing on your own spiritual condition at this time? How will you respond?

Consider the details Christ reveals about the churches, down to the activities of individuals. Do you believe Christ knows about your church? Does Christ know you are a member? Are you in His Book of Life? Does that assure you a place in the New Jerusalem? Note the greetings, they are all from Christ, and remember how Christ identifies himself. If you see any of these phrases in the remainder of the study you will know it is Christ himself.

# Revelation Chapter 4

We have finished the easy part of the study of Revelation. We now get a glimpse of God's throne room and the recognition of all that Jesus Christ has done for us. We gain a feeling for the authority given to Christ and why He alone deserves it. As chapter 4 opens we see God in his throne room seated on his throne in full control of all that is happening in the universe.

*1 After this, I looked and saw a door that opened into heaven. Then the voice that had spoken to me at first and that sounded like a trumpet said, "Come up here! I will show you what must happen next." (CEV)*

This is the same voice John heard in chapter 1. This is Christ inviting John to join Him in heaven to see what will happen in the future.

*2 Right then the Spirit took control of me, and there in heaven I saw a throne and someone sitting on it. (CEV)*

We see four places where John is "in the Spirit" in Revelation (1:10, 4:2, 17:3, 21:10). When John is "in the Spirit" the Holy Spirit is giving John a vision. John is being shown situations and events he could not have seen with human eyesight. It is amazing that John was able to recall and record the events as clearly as he did. True prophecy comes from God through the Holy Spirit (2 Peter 1:20,21)

56

**Revelation 1:10** On the Lord's Day I was in the Spirit, and I heard behind me a loud voice like a trumpet, (NIV)

**Revelation 4:2** At once I was in the Spirit, and there before me was a throne in heaven with someone sitting on it. (NIV)

**Revelation 17:3** Then the angel carried me away in the Spirit into a desert. There I saw a woman sitting on a scarlet beast that was covered with blasphemous names and had seven heads and ten horns. (NIV)

**Revelation 21:10** And he carried me away in the Spirit to a mountain great and high, and showed me the Holy City, Jerusalem, coming down out of heaven from God. (NIV)

*3 The one who was sitting there sparkled with precious stones of jasper and carnelian. A rainbow that looked like an emerald surrounded the throne. (CEV)*

Wow, that must have been a beautiful sight. Too bad we do not have a more detailed look at the throne of God.

*4 Twenty-four other thrones were in a circle around that throne. And on each of these thrones there was an elder dressed in white clothes and wearing a gold crown. (CEV)*

The twenty-four thrones and 24 elders probably represent the 12 tribes of Israel and the 12 apostles of Christ. Their white attire represents their righteousness and their golden crowns represent their authority. These 24 probably represent all the redeemed of God for all time. They represent all those in the family of God for all time. As one accepts Christ as their

Lord and Savior they become joint heirs with Christ in the family of God.

*5 Flashes of lighting and roars of thunder came out from the throne in the center of the circle. Seven torches, which are the seven spirits of god, were burning in front of the throne. (CEV)*

Lightning and thunder signify significant activities in Revelation. Something important is about to happen. Here we see God and the Holy Spirit but Jesus Christ has not yet appeared. Do you remember the lighting and thunder associated with Moses receiving the Ten Commandments on Mount Sinai (Exodus 19:16)? Lightning and thunder are often used to signify God's power and majesty (Psalm 77:18)

**Exodus 19:16 On the morning of the third day there was thunder and lightning, with a thick cloud over the mountain, and a very loud trumpet blast. Everyone in the camp trembled. (NIV)**

As we have seen before the "seven spirits of God" is another name for the Holy Spirit. In (Zechariah 4:2-6) we are told the seven lamps are the Holy Spirit.

*6 Also in front of the throne was something that looked like a glass sea, clear as crystal. Around the throne in the center were four living creatures covered front and back with eyes. (CEV)*

Glass as we know it did not exist in John's day, crystal clear glass was impossible to find at that time (1 Corinthians 13:12). The (what looked like) crystal clear glass signifies the importance and holiness of God.

**1 Corinthians 13:12 Now we see but a poor reflection as in a mirror; then we shall see face to face. Now I know in part; then I shall know fully, even as I am fully known. (NIV)**

It is refreshing to know we will eventually know the whole truth. Set aside will be our personal opinion, our misconceptions, our biases, our carryover from generations past, and our own arrogance. That will all be replaced with God's truth when we meet Christ. As attractive as knowing the truth is, it is offset by being fully known. Are there some things you would rather be left out of your life history?

*7 The first creature was like a lion, the second one was like a bull, the third one had the face of a human, and the fourth was like a flying eagle. (CEV)*

The four living creatures represent the qualities and character of God. Like the cherubim, they guard God's throne, lead others in worship, and proclaim Gods holiness. The animal like appearance of these four figures represents majesty and power (lion), faithfulness (ox), intelligence (man), and sovereignty (eagle). Ezekiel observed similar creatures in one of his visions (Ezekiel 1:5-10).

*8 Each of the four living creatures had six wings, and their bodies were covered with eyes. Day and night they never stopped singing, "Holy, holy, holy is the Lord, the all-powerful God, who was and is and is coming!" 9 The living creatures kept praising, honoring, and thanking the one who sits on the throne and who lives forever and ever. 10 At the same time the twenty-four elders knelt down before the one sitting on the throne. And as they worshiped the one who lives forever, they placed their crowns in front of the throne and said, 11 "Our Lord and God, you are worthy to receive glory, honor, and power. You created all things and by your decision they are and were created." (CEV)*

The importance of this chapter is summed up in verse 11. God caused the creation and sustaining of all things. There is no limitation to God's creation and power. So, what does that mean to you? Are you not created in God's image? Do you not have the Holy Spirit residing within you? So there is no God given limitations to what you can do or have. All your limitations are self generated! Only your lack of action limits you. Even wrong actions teach us things we need to know. Success or failure is the results of actions we take or fail to take.

# REVELATION CHAPTER 5

We were in the throne room of God with God sitting on the throne as we left chapter 4.

## The Scroll and the Lamb

*1 In the right hand of the one sitting on the throne I saw a scroll that had writing on the inside and on the outside. And it was sealed in seven places. (CEV)*

Office Depot, printers, computers, and all those things we use now for creating documents did not exist in John's day. They used long scrolls up to 30 feet in length to record large documents. These rolls of material were sealed with wax or clay to separate important parts of the document. A document that was sealed with an image/insignia could only be opened by authorized people. The scroll in God's hand contains the full account of what God has planned for our planet Earth. The seven seals signify the importance of the information contained in the scroll. The seals were placed along the scroll to indicate a different phase or section of the document much as we use subheadings.

*2 I saw a mighty angel ask with a loud voice, "Who is worthy to open the scroll and break its seals?" 3 No one in heaven or on earth or under the earth was able to open the scroll or see inside it. 4 I cried hard because no one was found worthy to open the scroll or see inside it. 5 Then one of the elders said to me, "Stop crying and look! The one who is called both the 'Lion for the Tribe of Judah' and 'King David's Great Descendent' has won the victory. He will open the book and its seven seals." (CEV)*

Remember the titles Christ was given in the letters to the churches. Only Jesus Christ has proved himself worthy to break the seals and open the scroll. By living the sinless life, giving his life for the sins of the world, rising from the dead and winning souls for God has qualified Christ to open the seals that reveal the future of Earth. The "Root of David" ties Christ back to fulfilling the promise of the Messiah in the Old Testament. The reference back to the Old Testament ties the 66 Books of the Bible together. We do not really understand the Bible until we understand all 66 Books.

*6 Then I looked and saw a Lamb standing in the center of the throne that was surrounded by the four living creatures and the elders. The Lamb looked as if it had once been killed. It had seven horns and seven eyes, which are the seven spirits of God, sent out to the earth. (CEV)*

The Lamb represents Christ's submission to God's will at His crucifixion. The Lion referenced in verse 5 indicates Christ's authority and power. When the elder called John to view the Lion John saw only the Lamb. Christ the Lamb was the perfect sacrifice for the sins of all mankind through all time. Christ the Lion is victorious over Satan only because of what the Lamb has already accomplished.

John saw the Lamb with the wounds Jesus received during his trial and crucifixion. John the Baptist called Jesus the Lamb of God (John 1:29). Before Christ's crucifixion lambs were used to sacrifice for sins. Christ's crucifixion was the final sacrifice for all sins for all time (Isaiah 53:7; Hebrews 10:1-18).

**Isaiah 53:7 He was oppressed and afflicted, yet he did not open his mouth; he was led like a lamb to the slaughter, and as a sheep before her shearers is silent, so he did not open his mouth. (NIV)**

Christ did not defend himself against the false charges that were brought against him.

Christ the sacrificial lamb is by no means weak; he was killed but now lives in God's strength and power.

*7 The Lamb went over and took the scroll from the right hand of the one who sat on the throne. 8 After he had taken it, the four living creatures and the twenty-four elders knelt down before him. Each of them had a harp and a gold bowl full of incense, which are the prayers of God's people. 9 Then they sang a new song, "You are worthy to receive the scroll and open its seals, because you were killed. And with your own blood you bought for God people from every tribe, language, nation, and race. 10 You let them become kings and serve God as priests, and they will rule on earth." (CEV)*

We have established the New Jerusalem where the believers will reside and the burning pit where the nonbelievers will reside. So what is there to reign over? Remember this "they will reign on the earth" and we will discuss it later.

Christ has purchased People from every tribe, language, people and nation and they are standing before God on his throne and praising Him. God's salvation has no limits; it is available for all people everywhere! Anyone who comes to God in repentance and faith is accepted by him and will be part of his kingdom. Don't allow prejudice or bias to keep you from sharing Christ with others. Christ welcomes all people into his kingdom.

Christ was slain, purchased souls with his blood, gathered them in a kingdom, made them priests and appointed them to reign on the earth. Christ has died and paid the penalty for all sin. Christ is now gathering souls into his kingdom. In the future these souls will reign with Christ. Praise God for all that has been done, what is being done, and what will be done for all that have faith in him. Does the future God promises give you the strength to resist the many temptations available today?

The believers praise Christ for bringing them into his kingdom and making them rulers and spiritual teachers over all the nations in the future. Before Christ our sinful nature prevented us from approaching God. Since we have been cleansed by the blood of Christ we have access to God. Do you take advantage of this outstanding resource? Do you turn all your troubles over to Christ? Christ gave his life to open the channels of blessing between God and mankind.

The counselor will answer all our questions and clarify any doubt that we may have. Our sinful nature will be no more. We will be accepted into the family of God.

Does this say that our minds will be opened to all things and all our disbeliefs will be replaced with true knowledge and enlightened understanding?

*11 As I looked, I heard the voices of a lot of angels around the throne and the voices of the living creatures and of the elders. There were millions and millions o them, (CEV)*

These angels bring messages (Luke 1:26-28), protect God's people (Daniel 6:22), offer encouragement (Genesis 16:7), give guidance (Exodus 14:19), bring punishment (2 Samuel 24:16), patrol the earth (Ezekiel 1:9-14) and fight the forces of evil (2 Kings 6:16-18; Revelation 20:1). When their work is done they will continually praise God for all that has been done.

*12 and they were saying in a loud voice, "The Lamb who was killed is worthy to receive power, riches, wisdom, strength, honor, glory, and praise." 13 Then I heard all beings in heaven and on the earth and under the earth and in the sea offer praise. Together, all of them were saying, "Praise, honor, glory, and strength forever and ever to the one who sits on the throne and to the Lamb!" 14 The four living creatures said "Amen," while the elders knelt down and worshiped. (CEV)*

Jesus Christ, the Lamb, is the only one worthy to open the scroll (the events of the future). Christ, not Satan, holds the future! Jesus Christ is in control and only he is worthy to set into action the events of the future that lead to the end of the world as we know it. There will be a New World and a New Jerusalem. We have much more to study about the New Jerusalem in later chapters.

# REVELATION CHAPTER 6

## Opening the Seven Seals

*1 At the same time that I saw the Lamb open the first of the seven seals, I heard one of the four living creatures shout with a voice like thunder. It said, "Come out!" (CEV)*

This is the first of three seven-part judgments. The seal judgments are things that are happening on Earth now. The seal judgments are limited to 1/4 of the world. The trumpets (chapter 8: 9) [Partial judgment 1/3], and the bowls (chapter 16) [Total judgment], are the other two. As each seal is opened, Christ the Lamb sets in motion events that will bring about the end of human history. This scroll is not completely opened until the seventh seal is broken (8:1). The contents of the scroll reveal mankind's depravity and portray God's authority over the events of human history.

*2 Then I saw a white horse. Its rider carried a bow and was given a crown. He had already won some victories, and he went out to win more. (CEV)*

The first four seals present four horses. These horses represent God's judgment of mankind's disobedience. We still have the disobedience that got Adam and Eve kicked out of paradise. Will we ever learn? The four horses are also found in Zechariah 6:1-8.

3 When the Lamb opened the second seal, I heard the second living creature say, "Come out!" 4 Then another horse came out. It was fiery red. And its rider was given power to take all peace from the earth, so that people would slaughter one another. He was also given a big sword. (CEV)

5 When the Lamb opened the third seal, I heard the third living creature say, "Come out!" Then I saw a black horse and its rider had a balance scale in one hand. 6 I heard what sounded like a voice from somewhere among the four living creatures. It said, "A quart of wheat will cost you a whole day's wages! Three quarts of barley will cost you a day's wages too. But don't ruin the olive oil or the wine." (CEV)

7 When the Lamb opened the fourth seal, I heard the voice of the fourth living creature say, "Come out!" 8 Then I saw a pale green horse. Its rider was named Death, and Death's Kingdom followed behind. They were given power over one fourth of the earth, and they could kill its people with swords, famines, diseases, and wild animals. (CEV)

We have a white horse, a red horse, a black horse and a pale horse. The white horse we would normally associate with Christ (Rev 19:11), but here the other horses are part of the

67

judgment so it is unlikely this horse is associated with Christ. The white horse is associated with war, we have seen plenty of war and there is no indication that we will not see even more war. These wars were bent on conquest, the conquering of nations with all their land. Past history documents huge shifts in land ownership or control. Examples of these are Israel conquering the promised land. Later we have the Babylonian, Medo-Persian, Grecian, and Roman Empires.

The red horse had the power to take peace from the Earth and make men slay each other. That sounds more like our wars of today. Although excessive population causes the need for more room, wars today seem to be about how nations treat their neighboring nations or how a nations threat to the rest of the world. I would suggest the Red horse is in full control today. How do you read it?

The black horse had the power to cause economic disruption and famine. I think we see that today with our economic recession. I guess your view of the economy today depends on whether you have a job/business or not. The black horse brings excessive prices as compared to a working persons earning. As our economy shifts to service industries we find more and more low paying jobs. This truly is the age of the entrepreneur, where we see excessive wealth contrasted to the working persons pay.

The pale horse represents death. This horse is followed closely by Hades, the underground abode of the dead in Greek mythology. The pain of losing a loved one is familiar to most people today. We either have lost a loved one or know someone who has lost a loved one. This horse will be with us until the end of our time.

These four horses and their riders are referred to as the four horsemen of the Apocalypse.

The seals judgments are for one fourth of the earth. Even with our extreme disobedience and damage to God's earth He is limiting these judgments to ¼ of the earth. In these early days of the judgments we still have time to repent and turn away from our sins. It should be apparent by now that it is not God who is causing these disasters it is mankind. God is using us to accomplish his judgments. These wars, murders, poverty, and deaths are all things that mankind has caused. We will find this pattern repeating through out the rest of Revelation.

*9 When the Lamb opened the fifth seal, I saw under the altar the souls of everyone who had been killed for speaking God's message and telling about their faith. (CEV)*

John saw under the altar of sacrifice the souls of those killed because of their belief in God. Their testimony had cost them their lives. If it were illegal to be a Christian, would there be enough evidence to convict you? In John's time there was a massive effort by the Roman Empire to rid the world of the Christian belief. They were similar to Hitler's attempt to end the Jewish race. This must have been a massive display of souls. Christians are called to be firm in what they believe. Only those who persevere to the end will be rewarded by God (Mark 13:13).

*10 They shouted, "Master, you are holy and faithful! How long will it be before you judge and punish the people of this earth who killed us?" 11 Then each of those who had been killed was given a white robe and told to rest for a little while. They had to wait until the complete number of the*

*Lord's other servants and followers would be killed. (CEV)*

The souls of the martyrs are eager for God to bring justice to the earth, but they were told to wait until their total was complete. I thought that age was over and there would be no more killings just because you are a Christian. Apparently killings for religious reasons are not over. The white robes represent their holiness. Note that God has singled them out for special honors; their sacrifice will not be forgotten. God promises justice for all who suffer for their faith. God wants everyone to have time to consider believing in Jesus as their Lord and Savior. These people that were killed because of their belief in Jesus Christ will rein with Christ during the 1000 year period when Satan is bound in the bottomless pit.

*12 When I saw the Lamb open the sixth seal, I looked and saw a great earthquake. The sun turned as dark as sackcloth, and the moon became as red as blood. (CEV)*

The sixth seal brings us back to the earth we know. The first five judgments were directed to particular functions. This judgment, however, is universal. The whole world is afraid when the earth itself is in danger.

*13 The stars in the sky fell to earth, just like figs shaken loose by a windstorm. 14 Then the sky was rolled up like a scroll, and all mountains and islands were moved from their places. 15 The kings of the earth, its famous people, and its military leaders hid in caves or behind rocks in the mountains. They hid there together with the rich and the powerful and with all the slaves and free people. 16 Then they shouted to the mountains and the rocks, "Fall on us! Hide us from the one who sits on the throne and from the anger of the Lamb. 17 That terrible day has come! God and the Lamb will show their anger, and who can face it?" (CEV)*

This is the first indication that something drastic happened to the Earth! Whatever caused this disaster was due to the activities of mankind. Is this the first crucifixion of Earth by man? When God sets things right, and lets Earth continue, how can anyone not believe in God? Are the Christians removed from the Earth now? If the Christians are removed, who is left on the Earth? What will happen when only non-believers are left on the Earth? Will greed prevail? Will self-interest be the only thing limiting humankind's action? (Matthew 24:29-31)

We are living in a time when man can destroy the earth. Yes, we can crucify God's earth as we did Jesus! For the first time in human history, with the atomic age, mankind has the ability to destroy the earth. If a carbon bomb were to be exploded it would knock the earth out of orbit and cause the stars to seem to fall from the sky. If you will note carefully the judgments are things we do to each other. The wars, the pollution, etc. are all things we do to each other. I believe that when God promised Noah that he would not cause the world to flood again, it was a statement that he would not destroy the earth again. I believe God wants every human being to come to him, and that the only thing that will end his patience is the act of man in the destruction of earth. At that time he will intervene and set things right again. It sure is nice to have a loving God!

# REVELATION CHAPTER 7

*1 After this I saw four angels standing at the four corners of the earth, holding back the four winds of the earth to prevent any wind from blowing on the land or on the sea or on any tree. (NIV)*

Remember in chapter six where we experienced man's first crucifixion of the earth.

**Rev 6:12 I watched as he opened the sixth seal. There was a great earthquake. The sun turned black like sackcloth made of goat hair, the whole moon turned blood red, 13 and the stars in the sky fell to earth, as late figs drop from a fig tree when shaken by a strong wind. 14 The sky receded like a scroll, rolling up, and every mountain and island was removed from its place. (NIV)**

*2 Then I saw another angel coming up from the east, having the seal of the living God. He called out in a loud voice to the four angels who had been given power to harm the land and the sea: (NIV)*

The seal on a person (slave) identified the owner of that person. The seal on a document (scroll) identified the authority that had committed to protect/honor that document. After the first destruction of the earth God's people will be identified by a seal. Before the first destruction of the earth your conduct identified you as a Christian. As a Christian you have been sealed and guarantied. God's people and

Satan's people will not have a visible identification until the first destruction of the earth.

The special seal that God identifies His people gives you an idea of how important you are to God. If you are sealed by God Satan cannot harm your spiritual soul. Satan can harm your physical body and cause you to suffer pain.

Is this mark a physical mark or is this the way we conduct ourselves? Can people tell you are a Christian by the way you conduct yourself? My view is that before the first crucifixion of the earth your actions determined if you are in God's family. After the first crucifixion of earth people will have a visible seal that determines if they belong to God or Satan.

*3 "Do not harm the land or the sea or the trees until we put a seal on the foreheads of the servants of our God." (NIV)*

After God puts His seal on His follower's to protect them from the Trumpet judgments Satan places his seal on his follower's forehead or right hand. Having a seal meant that you were either one of God's follower's or Satan's follower's. Does this give you a feeling of how important you are to God?

*4 Then I heard the number of those who were sealed: 144,000 from all the tribes of Israel. 5 From the tribe of Judah 12,000 were sealed, from the tribe of Reuben 12,000, from the tribe of Gad 12,000, 6 from the tribe of Asher 12,000, from the tribe of Naphtali 12,000, from the tribe of Manasseh 12,000, 7 from the tribe of Simeon 12,000, from the tribe of Levi*

*12,000, from the tribe of Issachar 12,000, 8 from the tribe of Zebulun 12,000, from the tribe of Joseph 12,000, from the tribe of Benjamin 12,000. (NIV)*

Have you ever attended a "Jews for Christ" service? You may never be invited to their service; but, if you are invited do not miss the opportunity. I was invited at one time and it was an outstanding service.

The Bible puts a lot of meaning to numbers, the number 12 X 12 X 1000 (144,000) symbolizes completeness. After man's crucifixion of the earth and God's intervention there was no question about the existence of God. These 144,000 are conversions among the Jews that have been faithful to their tribes of the nation of Israel. The majority of Jews have in one way or another separated themselves from the original heritage of the Jews. This separation happened through the adulteration of tribal blood line in any of a multitude of ways. These that have received the seal of God will receive their reward of eternal life with God. Remember, Christ promised he would not loose one of these given to him by God.

This is not saying that 144,000 individuals must be sealed before the persecution comes, but that when persecution begins, the faithful will have already been sealed (marked by God), and they will remain true to him until the end.

| Old Testament Tribes of Israel | Revelation Tribes of Israel |
|---|---|
| Reuben | Reuben |
| Simeon | Simeon |
| Levi | Levi |
| Judah | Judah |

| Zebulun | Zebulun |
|---------|---------|
| Issachar | Issachar |
| Dan | Manasseh |
| Gad | Gad |
| Asher | Asher |
| Naphtali | Naphtali |
| Joseph | Joseph |
| Benjamin | Benjamin |

Dan was eliminated because of rebellion and idolatry. Joseph's son Manasseh took Dan's place. Joseph's other son Ephraim was not listed because of his rebellion. Have you ever experienced a rebellious son? Even Joseph's family has that problem. Levi was included for the faithfulness

*9 After this I looked and there before me was a great multitude that no one could count, from every nation, tribe, people and language, standing before the throne and in front of the Lamb. They were wearing white robes and were holding palm branches in their hands. (NIV)*

Who is this great multitude? While some interpreters identify it as the martyrs described in 6:9, it may also be the same group as the 144,000 just mentioned (7:4-8). The 144,000 were sealed by God before the great time of persecution; the great multitude was brought to eternal life, as God had promised. Before, they were being prepared; now, they are victorious. This multitude in heaven is composed of all those who remained faithful to God throughout the generations. No true believer ever need worry about which group he or she will be in. God includes and protects each of us, and we are guaranteed a place in his presence. However; I believe this is the saints gathered before God and His Jesus. Do you recognize yourself in this crowd?

*10 And they cried out in a loud voice: "Salvation belongs to our God, who sits on the throne, and to the Lamb." (NIV)*

Salvation comes from God through Christ. As sinners we cannot come into God presence without first having applied Christ's cleansing blood. Christ gave his life so we can come within Gods domain. We try many foolish ways to try to cover our sins. We often blame others; will we ever grow up and take responsibility for our own action? We do good deeds; salvation is not about what we do for God it is about what God has done for us.

The people in heaven praise God and know salvation comes from God and Christ. The penalty for sin is death, we will all die; but, our souls belong to God through the redeeming blood of Christ. We will be spared the second death, which is separation from God and Christ.

*11 All the angels were standing around the throne and around the elders and the four living creatures. They fell down on their faces before the throne and worshiped God, (NIV)*

The four living creatures represent the qualities and characteristics of God. They guard God's throne forever and ever. They lead others in worship. They proclaim God's holiness. The appearances of these four creatures are majesty and power (Lion), faithfulness (Ox), intelligence (Man), and Sovereignty (Eagle). Ezekiel saw four similar creatures in Ezekiel 1:5-10.

*12 saying: "Amen! Praise and glory and wisdom and thanks and honor and power and strength be to our God for ever and ever. Amen!" 13 Then one of the elders asked me, "These in white robes-- who are they, and where did they come from?" 14 I answered, "Sir, you know." And he said, "These are they who have come out of the great tribulation; they have washed their robes and made them white in the blood of the Lamb. (NIV)*

Some believe the great tribulation refers to the Roman Empire's persecution of the Christians during the reign of Rome. Some believe it refers to the suffering of Christians throughout the generations. Others believe there is a time of intense tribulation yet to come. I believe we need to let God tell what is next by paying attention to what comes next in our study of Revelation.

Can you imagine what a mess you would make if you soaked your white attire in blood? You would no doubt have to replace it and throw the stained one away. But the blood of Jesus is the greatest purifier because it removes the stain of sin. In Revelation white signifies sinlessness or holiness.

*15 Therefore, "they are before the throne of God and serve him day and night in his temple; and he who sits on the throne will spread his tent over them. 16 Never again will they hunger; never again will they thirst. The sun will not beat upon them, or any scorching heat. 17 For the Lamb at the center of the throne will be their shepherd;*

*he will lead them to springs of living water. And God will wipe away every tear from their eyes." (NIV)*

God will not only provide for all our needs, God will take away all our sorrow. There will be no more death, sickness, hunger, pain or suffering of any kind.

We start this chapter with all believers receiving a seal to protect them during the coming tribulation and suffering. We close this chapter seeing the believers with God in Heaven, they are serving God before God's throne.

# REVELATION CHAPTER 8

*1 When he opened the seventh seal, there was silence in heaven for about half an hour. 2 And I saw the seven angels who stand before God and to them were given seven trumpets. (NIV)*

This is the start of the trumpet judgments, they like the seal judgments are partial judgments. As the seal judgments were for 1/4 of the earth the trumpet judgments are for 1/3 of the earth. At the seventh trumpet judgment the bowl judgments will be introduced. The bowl judgment unlike the seal and trumpet judgment are total judgments (Revelation 11:15 and 16:1-21). The half an hour pause in Heaven signifies we are entering a more serious judgment than we witnessed in the seal judgments.

*3 Another angel, who had a golden censer, came and stood at the altar. He was given much incense to offer, with the prayers of all the saints, on the golden altar before the throne. (NIV)*

Some churches still use incense in their worship service. The sweet smelling smoke drifting upward is supposed to represent the prayer of the saints ascending to God.

*4 The smoke of the incense, together with the prayers of the saints, went up before God from the angel's hand. 5 Then the angel took the censer, filled it with fire from the altar, and hurled it on the earth; and there came peals of thunder, rumblings, flashes of lightning and an earthquake. 6 Then the seven angels who had the seven trumpets prepared to sound them. (NIV)*

The trumpet blast are used to:

* Warn that judgment is certain,
* Call the forces of good and evil to battle,
* Announce the return of the King, the Messiah.

We must make sure our faith is fixed on Jesus Christ.

*7 The first angel sounded his trumpet, and there came hail and fire mixed with blood, and it was hurled down upon the earth. A third of the earth was burned up, a third of the trees were burned up, and all the green grass was burned up. (NIV)*

Notice that these judgments are much more severe than the seal judgments. One third of the earth was burned up. I wonder what happened to California during this fire storm. Our renewable resource, trees, received a major hit. All the grass was burned up; they didn't even spare the lawns. We have never witnessed such a loss to fire and I hope we never will. I am glade we only have to contend with the seal judgments. We will not be here when the trumpet judgments start.

*8 The second angel sounded his trumpet, and something like a huge mountain, all ablaze, was thrown into the sea. A third of the sea turned into blood, 9 a third of the living creatures in the sea died, and a third of the ships were destroyed. (NIV)*

What mountain is this? One third of the sea was turned to blood. Can you imagine what a mess that would make and how difficult it would be to clean up. One third of the creatures in the sea died at the same time. What a mess that would be. One can almost smell the rotting fish along the sea shore. One third of the ships at sea were destroyed with all their cargo. What a blow to the world transportation and financial systems.

*10 The third angel sounded trumpet, and a great star, blazing like a torch, fell from the sky on a third of the rivers and on the springs of water—11 the name of the star is Wormwood. A third of the waters turned bitter, and many people died from the waters that had become bitter. (NIV)*

We have had some major water pollution problems; but, nothing of this magnitude. I wonder what the price of water will be then. Will water be more expensive than gasoline? We have had bad water in some aired areas of the world but never a third of the water supply. We have been very destructive with the earth's resources but this is much worse. Remember we will later establish that these disasters are due to mankind's activities. This makes our pollution problems seem small compared to what they will be during the trumpet judgments. If you remove all of God's people from the earth what is left to protect the earth?

*12 The fourth angel sounded his trumpet, and a third of the sun was struck, a third of the moon, and a third of the stars, so that a third of them turned dark. A third of the day was without light, and also a third of the night. (NIV)*

I love to walk on a cool moon lit night. I can't imagine one third of the day and night without light. Some people get depressed on rainy days and Mondays. Can you imagine what it will be like with light for only one third of the day and night?

Note that only 1/3 of the earth is damaged by these trumpet judgments. This is only a partial judgment from God. God's full judgment will be coming with the bowl judgments.

*13 As I watched, I heard an eagle that was flying in midair call out in a loud voice: "Woe! Woe! Woe to the inhabitants of the earth, because of the trumpet blasts about to be sounded by the other three angels!" (NIV)*

Remember after the rapture that occurred at the end of Chapter 6 there only remained non-believers. When God intervened and set the earth right there was no doubt that God exist and many became believers. These new believers are marked with the seal of God while the nonbelievers are marked with the seal of Satan.

The Old Testament used the image of a vulture to show speed of destruction (1:8 Habakkuk). The eagle here is flying over the earth warning people about the things that are about to happen. The people with God's seal may have physical damage but their spirit is protected by God and will receive no damage. The people with Satan's seal will have both physical and spiritual damage.

82

As we wait impatiently remember the Saints that ask God how much longer they must wait for judgment. They were told their number was not yet complete and that they must wait a little longer. God has a plan that will become apparent later, but things happen at God's timing not our own. We need to thank God for giving us time to accept his teaching and conform to his way of conducting our lives. We must use our time to help others turn to Jesus Christ for their salvation.

# REVELATION CHAPTER 9

*1 The fifth angel sounded his trumpet, and I saw a star that had fallen from the sky to the earth. The star was given the key to the shaft of the Abyss. (NIV)*

Let us recap a little bit. We have completed the seal judgments, most of which is happening now. The seal judgments ended in what seemed to be the end of the earth but God intervened and the earth survived. The believers were harvested from the earth leaving only the non-believers on earth. Now there is positive proof there is a God, yet not everyone is a believer. How can we be so hardheaded?

We have now entered the trumpet judgments. The size of the earth seems to have changed. After the first trumpet 1/3 of the earth was burned up, a third of the trees were burned up, and all the grass was burned up.

After the second trumpet a huge mountain all ablaze was thrown into the sea. A third of the sea turned to blood, a third of the creatures in the sea died, and a third of the ships were destroyed.

After the third trumpet a great star, blazing like a torch, fell from the sky on a third of the rivers and all the springs of water. The stars name was wormwood. A third of the waters turned bitter, and many people died from the waters that had turned bitter.

After the fourth trumpet a third of the sun was struck, a third of the moon, and a third of the stars so that a third of them turned dark.

And here we have the fifth trumpet sounding and a star falls from the sky to the earth. The star is given the key to the shaft of the Abyss.

I don't know what this star that fell from the sky is. Some say it is Satan the fallen angel. Some say it is Christ. Some say it is a good angel. The key to the Abyss (bottomless pit) is normally held by Christ (1:17, 18). It is way too early for Christ to be on the earth. This being, whoever, is still under the control and authority of God. The Abyss is the place for Satan and all his demons (Luke 8:31).

*2 When he opened the Abyss, smoke rose from it like the smoke from a gigantic furnace. The sun and sky were darkened by the smoke from the Abyss. 3 And out of the smoke locusts came down upon the earth, and were given power like that of scorpions of the earth. (NIV)*

Joel's description of the locust plague indicated God's coming judgment. In the agrarian society of the Old Testament the locusts were symbols of total destruction because they ate all the vegetation. Here they are demons called to torture all people that are non-believers. The demons could only torture people for five months. This limitation proves they are under God's control.

These demons, most likely, are fallen angels ruled by Satan. Satan did not create them but somehow they fell into Satan's control. All creation is by God! God limits what they can do and how long they can do it. These demons purpose is to prevent, distort, or destroy people's faith in God. They are corrupt and degenerate. They have no redeeming qualities even their appearance reflect the distortion of their spirit. We must avoid any involvement with demonic forces or with the occult.

85

*4 They were told not to harm the grass of the earth or any plant or tree, but only those people who did not have the seal of God on their foreheads. 5 They were not given power to kill them, but only to torture them for five months. And the agony they suffered was like that of the sting of a scorpion when it strikes a man. 6 During those days men will seek death, but will not find it; they will long to die, but death will elude them. 7 The locusts looked like horses prepared for battle. On their heads they wore something like crowns of gold, and their faces resembled human faces. 8 Their hair was like women's hair, and their teeth were like lions' teeth. 9 They had breastplates like breastplates of iron, and the sound of their wings was like the thundering of many horses and chariots rushing into battle. 10 They had tails and stings like scorpions, and in their tails they had power to torment people for five months. 11 They had as king over them the angel of the Abyss, whose name in Hebrew is Abaddon, and in Greek, Apollyon. (NIV)*

Abaddon in Hebrew, and Apollyon in Greek, mean destroyer. This is the first Woe, there are two more to come. John may be trying to show that those who do not believe in Jesus Christ worship only a demon. Only those people that wore the seal of Satan were stung. No one with the Seal of God was damaged.

*12 The first woe is past; two other woes are yet to come. 13 The sixth angel sounded his trumpet, and I heard a voice coming from the horns of the golden altar that is before God. (NIV)*

The Old Testament altar in the temple had four projections, one on each corner, and these were called horns of the altar Exodus 27:2).

*14 It said to the sixth angel who had the trumpet, "Release the four angels who are bound at the great river Euphrates." (NIV)*

These angels are fallen angels or demons. They will be exceedingly evil and destructive. Note they are released by God not their own free will. They will only do what God allows them to do.

*15 And the four angels who had been kept ready for this very hour and day and month and year were released to kill a third of mankind. (NIV)*

Here when the sixth trumpet is sounded evil forces kill 1/3 of the population of earth. In Revelation 6:7, 8 only one quarter of the earth's population were killed. Even more would have been killed if God had not set limits on the destruction.

*16 The number of the mounted troops was two hundred million. I heard their number. (NIV)*

Today a million man Army is a huge Army that requires huge resources to sustain and train. A two hundred million man Army suggest a much larger population than exists now, and an economy that can support that size of an Army. This huge army, led by the four demons, will be sent out to destroy one-third of the earth's population. But the judgment is still not complete.

*17 The horses and riders I saw in my vision looked like this: Their breastplates were fiery red, dark blue, and yellow as sulfur. The heads of the horses resembled the heads of lions, and out of their mouths came fire, smoke and sulfur. 18 A third of mankind was killed by the three plagues of fire, smoke and sulfur that came out of their mouths. (NIV)*

Sounds like something from a horror flick to me. Can you imagine every third person you know being killed? Of course you must remember if you have the seal of God on your forehead you will not be harmed.

*19 The power of the horses was in their mouths and in their tails; for their tails were like snakes, having heads with which they inflict injury. 20 The rest of mankind that were not killed by these plagues still did not repent of the work of their hands; they did not stop worshiping demons, and idols of gold, silver, bronze, stone and wood-- idols that cannot see or hear or walk. 21 Nor did they repent of their murders, their magic arts, their sexual immorality or their thefts. (NIV)*

These judgments are so harsh that they are beyond our comprehension, they are directed at non-believers, yet none repent and turn to God. We are born with the Holy Spirit within all of us. The Holy Spirit guides as to how we must conduct ourselves. As we, first timidly then aggressively, resist the urging of the Holy Spirit the spirits influence is weakened until it no longer influences our behavior. I am sure you know people like that today. Our fall into immorality does not happen over night but one small step at a time. First we find that not telling the complete truth keeps us from unpleasant things. Once we accept that, lying becomes second nature to us. Sexual immorality has a similar progression first a tease, then a touch, and the cycle spins out of control.

As we allow sin to influence our lives we find ourselves avoiding our religious friends and becoming closer to our sinful friends. What's the saying? Birds of a feather flock together? Well that describes us also; we tend to gather with people of the same mindset as our own. Temptation leads to sin, sin leads to habit, and then sinful habit leads to death. That death is the second death, the separation from God. To think you could never become this evil is the first step toward a hard heart. Acknowledge your need to confess your sin before God.

These people have witnessed God's power as He has restored the world they destroyed in chapter 6. Still they will not repent!

# REVELATION CHAPTER 10

*1 Then I saw another mighty angel coming down from heaven. He was robed in a cloud, with a rainbow above his head; his face was like the sun, and his legs were like fiery pillars. 2 He was holding a little scroll, which lay open in his hand. He planted his right foot on the sea and his left foot on the land; (NIV)*

This is the second scroll we see in Revelation. The first scroll with the seal of God discloses the future of the earth. The first scroll tells as much of the future of the earth as we need to know now. This second scroll seems to make more of a statement about how this is going to make John feel. However, the content of the second small scroll is not given.

*3 and he gave a loud shout like the roar of a lion. When he shouted, the voices of the seven thunders spoke. 4 And when the seven thunders spoke, I was about to write; but I heard a voice from heaven say, "Seal up what the seven thunders have said and do not write it down." (NIV)*

The information in the seven thunders is not for us yet. Apparently our tendency to speak out of turn continues with the seven thunders in that they gave information that we are not prepared to receive yet. John has been prevented from revealing what was said by the seven thunders. Man has always wanted to know what will happen tomorrow. God tells us all we need to know about the future in Revelation. The prophet Daniel was also given some visions that were not to be revealed (Daniel 12:9). Jesus told the apostles the time for the end is known only by the Father (Mark 13:32, 33). God has revealed all we need to know to live for him now. In our desire to be ready for the end, we must not place more emphasis on speculation about the last days than on living for God while we wait.

*5 Then the angel I had seen standing on the sea and on the land raised his right hand to heaven. 6 And he swore by him who lives for ever and ever, who created the heavens and all that is in them, the earth and all that is in it, and the sea and all that is in it, and said, "There will be no more delay! (NIV)*

Wow, this is it, no more stalling around; we are ready for the final total judgment. This judgment includes all that is in the earth and sea. The seventh trumpet will bring on the bowl judgments which are the total judgments. We are about to see the end of our present world; but, there will a New Earth and New Jerusalem (the holy city of God). God's truth will prevail!

*7 But in the days when the seventh angel is about to sound his trumpet, the mystery of God will be accomplished, just as he announced to his servants the prophets." (NIV)*

All prophecy will be fulfilled when God's plan for humanity is revealed. The end of the age will have arrived (11:15; Ephesians 1:9, 10).

*8 Then the voice that I had heard from heaven spoke to me once more: "Go, take the scroll that lies open in the hand of the angel who is standing on the sea and on the land." 9 So I went to the angel and asked him to give me the little scroll. He said to me, "Take it and eat it. It will turn your stomach sour, but in your mouth it will be as sweet as honey." 10 I took the little scroll from the angel's hand and ate it. It tasted as sweet as honey in my mouth, but when I had eaten it, my stomach turned sour. (NIV)*

The prophet Ezekiel had a similar experience as John about revealing the future to the nation of Israel (Ezekiel 3:1). Ezekiel's message brought destruction to Israel just as John's will bring destruction to the Earth. God's work brings encouragement to believers but also regret for the harm to come to the non-believers.

*11 Then I was told, "You must prophesy again about many peoples, nations, languages and kings." (NIV)*

# REVELATION CHAPTER 11

*1 I was given a reed like a measuring rod and was told, "Go and measure the temple of God and the altar, and count the worshipers there. (NIV)*

The temple of God is probably some kind of worship area because there will be no temple in the New Jerusalem (21:22). John's measurements show there will be protection for believers and there will be room for every believer who remains faithful.

*2 But exclude the outer court; do not measure it, because it has been given to the Gentiles. They will trample on the holy city for 42 months. (NIV)*

Is God saying the outer court will be open to all who desire to be there? After all this, God is still willing to accept all that come! What an Awesome God! Those worshiping inside the worship area will be protected spiritually, those outside will have 42 months (3 1/2 Years) to confess their sins and accept Christ as their Lord and Savior.

*3 And I will give power to my two witnesses, and they will prophesy for 1,260 days, clothed in sackcloth." (NIV)*

The 1260 days is 42 months or 3 1/2 years. These two witnesses remind us of Moses and Elijah. They were two of God's mighty prophets. Moses called plagues down on Egypt (Exodus 8-11). Elijah defeated the prophets of Baal (1

Kings18). Moses and Elijah explained to Jesus the alternatives to crucifixion at the transfiguration (Mathew 17:1-7)

Well I am setting you up for a pivotal surprise. We see here where God intervenes into the lives of people to accomplish his goals. That is not what my God is all about? My God is a loving God that allows me free choice in all I do. When I sin and ask God for forgiveness I receive it. That does not mean I do not have to deal with the results of my sin. I am forgiven but still responsible for all that I do.

What is Elijah telling us here? Is he saying that you not only have to be persistent, you must believe, and also expect to receive what you desire? Now I think you understand why you needed to read about Elijah. Was the Law of Attraction working for Elijah? Seven in the Bible implies complete or full or sufficient. Elijah sent his servants back to see if the rain was coming until there was a sign that the rain was coming. No less than abundant rain was even considered. Do you have that kind of faith in the completion of your desires?

In the book of revelation, numbers have symbolic rather than literal meaning. The 42 months or 1,260 days equal 3 ½ years. As half of the perfect number 7, 3½ can indicate incompletion, imperfection, or even evil. Notice the events predicted for this time period: there is trouble (Daniel 12:7), the holy city is trampled (11:2), the woman takes refuge in the desert 12:6), and the devil-inspired beast exercises his authority 13:5). Some commentators link the 3 ½ years with the period of famine in the days of Elijah (Luke 4:25; James 5:17). Since Malachi predicted the return of Elijah before the Last Judgment (Malachi 4:5), and since events in Daniel and Revelation pave the way for the second coming, perhaps John was making this connection. It is possible, of course, that the 3 ½ years are literal. If so, we will clearly recognize when 3 ½ years are over! Whether symbolic or literal, however, they indicate that evil's reign will have a definite end.

*4 These are the two olive trees and the two lampstands that stand before the Lord of the earth. 5 If anyone tries to harm them, fire comes from their mouths and devours their enemies. This is how anyone who wants to harm them must die. 6 These men have power to shut up the sky so that it will not rain during the time they are prophesying; and they have power to turn the waters into blood and to strike the earth with every kind of plague as often as they want. 7 Now when they have finished their testimony, the beast that comes up from the Abyss will attack them, and overpower and kill them. (NIV)*

Remember the lamp stands in chapter 1. They were churches. These two churches must be very powerful churches. The pastors of these two churches must be prophets that have the ability to call down fire to devour anyone who wants to harm them. The plagues they are capable of controlling are like the powers of God that Moses demonstrated. This beast that overpowers them must be Satan or an agent of Satan because they come out of the Abyss.

*8 Their bodies will lie in the street of the great city, which is figuratively called Sodom and Egypt, where also their Lord was crucified. 9 For three and a half days men from every people, tribe, language and nation will gaze on their bodies and refuse them burial. 10 The inhabitants of the earth will gloat over them and will celebrate by sending each other gifts, because these two prophets had tormented those who live on the earth. (NIV)*

Unbelievers were quick to celebrate the failure of these moral giants. There was no one remaining to correct their wicked way. They were free to do as they pleased. There was no one to urge repentance and acceptance of Christ. They hated Christ and his followers (1 John 3:13). When you obey Christ and take a stand against sin, be prepared to experience the world's hatred. Remember that the reward waiting you in heaven far exceeds any suffering that you face now.

*11 But after the three and a half days a breath of life from God entered them, and they stood on their feet, and terror struck those who saw them. 12 Then they heard a loud voice from heaven saying to them, "Come up here." And they went up to heaven in a cloud, while their enemies looked on. 13 At that very hour there was a severe earthquake and a tenth of the city collapsed. Seven thousand people were killed in the earthquake, and the survivors were terrified and gave glory to the God of heaven. 14 The second woe has passed; the third woe is coming soon. (NIV)*

Even the non-believers recognized this as an act of God. Unlike previous judgments, here some gave glory of God in heaven.

*15 The seventh angel sounded his trumpet, and there were loud voices in heaven, which said: "The kingdom of the world has become the kingdom of our Lord and of his Christ, and he will reign for ever and ever." (NIV)*

The arrival of the King of Kings sets the stage for the final battle between good and evil. The time for repentance has ended; it is too late to switch sides now. The coming judgments will be complete there will be no more partial judgments. God is in full control and unleashes his full anger against the evil world that refuses to turn to him (9:20, 21). God's anger will not be denied any longer; there will be no escape.

*16 And the twenty-four elders, who were seated on their thrones before God, fell on their faces and worshiped God, (NIV)*

These elders are the same ones we discussed before that represents the 12 tribes of Israel in the Old Testament and the 12 apostles in the New Testament. These 24 represent all the redeemed of God for all time. They represent all that have become part of God's family. All the redeemed of the Lord are worshiping God.

*17 saying: "We give thanks to you, Lord God Almighty, the One who is and who was, because you have taken your great power and have begun to reign. 18 The nations were angry; and your wrath has come. The time has come for judging the dead, and for rewarding your servants the prophets and your saints and those who reverence your name, both small and great-- and for destroying those who destroy the earth." (NIV)*

There are pivotal passages in Revelation and we see one here. We see at the end of verse 18 the statement "destroying those who destroy the earth" up until now some people believed God was causing the destruction of the Earth; but, here it is clearly stated that we are destroying the Earth and God is witnessing our actions. Sounds like God will destroy the non-believers who have been destroying His Earth.

Here is our pivotal phrase **"and for destroying those who destroy the earth."** So all these things that looked like God was causing we brought upon ourselves. God used us to bring about the judgments recorded in Revelation. This suggests the environmentalists are on the right track. Perhaps not focused on the correct actions but at least headed in the right direction.

When you become a Christian you do good deeds out of the love of God. We do not expect direct rewards for these deeds. If we received direct rewards for each good deed we would soon start doing good deeds for greedy reasons which would lead to our corruption. While it is true that God will reward us for our earthly deeds our greatest reward is eternal life with God (20:12).

*19 Then God's temple in heaven was opened, and within his temple was seen the ark of his covenant. And there came flashes of lightning, rumblings, and peals of thunder, an earthquake and a great hailstorm. (NIV)*

Although these instructions were given to the people of Israel, we have been grafted into the family of God. Do you think it is time we took our Christian beliefs to heart and start doing what we are supposed to do? Are you doing all you can?

# REVELATION CHAPTER 12

Before we start Revelation 12 let us review what we have studied this far. In Revelation 1 we were introduced to the risen Christ and his relationship with the churches. Revelation 2 and 3 were instructions to the universal church. A number of things that were destructive to the church were listed, and a number of things that should be encouraged were listed. These instructions, although they were specifically addressed to individual churches, are important instructions for all churches today.

In Revelation 4 and 5 we are introduced to God's throne and the scroll that holds the secret future of the earth and all its inhabitants. We found that our Lord Jesus Christ is the only one worthy of breaking the seal to allow the scroll to reveal the future of Earth and Heaven.

In Revelation 6 we see the first of the seven part judgments. These judgments seem like the things that are happening to our Earth today. These judgments are limited to one quarter of the earth. These judgments are terminated by what seems to be the end of the earth. It would seem like the earth is knocked out of its orbit, every mountain and island being removed from their place. With the advent of the Atomic age, man now has the capability to destroy the Earth. Is this Man's first crucifixion of God's Earth as man has crucified God's Son Jesus Christ? Something happens and the Earth is allowed to continue. We have to go to Matthew 24:30-31 to see what happened to allow the earth to continue.

In Revelation 7 we see God's protection of his people; everyone that has confirmed their belief in Jesus Christ as their Lord and Savior is protected from coming judgments.

In Revelation 8 and 9 we see the beginning of the seven Trumpet judgments. The judgments here are harsher than before, but are limited to one third of the Earth. We see some indications here that the Earth is much larger than our Earth today. We see things like a million man Army and two hundred million mounted troops. The intervention at the end of Revelation 6 make it known that there is a single God that has the power to correct man's actions against the Earth, however they continue their sinful ways and the worship of false gods.

In Revelation 10 we are told that what the seven Thunders spoke was to be sealed up and not revealed at this time. Daniel was instructed not to reveal words until the time of the end in Daniel 12:9. John was told to eat a small scroll that represented his prophesy against many peoples, nations, languages and kings. The knowledge was sweet to John but the horror of the judgments turned his stomach sour.

In Revelation 11 John is required to measure the size of the temple of God and Alter and count the worshipers there. The results were not reveled yet; we will see some significant sizes later. We have the story of the two olive trees and lamp stands. So far we have been told about some very dreadful judgments and most people assume they are caused by God. Here we discover a pivotal statement "destroying those who destroy the earth." This shows us that it is not God's destruction of his Earth but man's destruction of God's Earth. Here again we realize that man not only crucified God's son Jesus Christ but also God's Earth.

In Revelation 12 thru 14 we see the Birth of Jesus Christ and the great conflict between God and Satan. The birth and life of our Jesus Christ, His death and Resurrection, are the most important single event in mankind's existence. Without Christ sacrifice for our sins there is no one, except Jesus Christ, that has lived a sinless life. Without Jesus there could be no Book of Life and no way that we could gain access to the New Jerusalem.

*1 A great and wondrous sign appeared in heaven: a woman clothed with the sun, with the moon under her feet and a crown of twelve stars on her head. (NIV)*

The seventh trumpet judgment (11:15) announced God's kingdom is now on earth. You can expect some changes on earth! Before that happens John shows us some of the conflict between God and the forces of evil, Satan and his followers (12-14). In these chapters we will see the source of all sin, evil, persecution, and suffering. The nature of sin will be exposed for all to view. Finally the bowl judgments will be completed (15:1-16:21). Satan is revealed in all his wickedness.

This devout Jew named Mary is about to give birth to our Lord and Savior Jesus Christ.

We know the woman as Mary the mother of Jesus. God's faithful people had been waiting for the Messiah. Mary represents all of God's faithful people. The twelve stars represent the twelve tribes of Israel. We see in Romans (Romans 9:4 - 5) where God set apart the Jews for himself. The Jewish nation gave birth to our Lord and Savior. Their responsibility is to bring the truth about God to the people of the earth. That is kind of hard to do if you do not believe in Jesus Christ as your Lord and Savior.

*3 Then another sign appeared in heaven: an enormous red dragon with seven heads and ten horns and seven crowns on his heads. 4 His tail swept a third of the stars out of the sky and flung them to the earth.*

*The dragon stood in front of the woman who was about to give birth, so that he might devour her child the moment it was born. 5 She gave birth to a son, a male child, who will rule all the nations with an iron scepter. And her child was snatched up to God and to his throne. (NIV)*

The red dragon is Satan and he is attempting to kill Jesus Christ. The third of the stars from the sky suggest Satan has managed to get one third of God's angels to follow him. If Satan can convince one third of God's angels to follow him do you see what a powerful force you are up against in your attempt to remain faithful? The woman is Mary the mother of Jesus Christ. Remember Joseph was told to take Mary and Jesus to Egypt until it was safe for them to return. King Herod caused all the children under two years old to be killed. However Joseph, Mary and Jesus were already in Egypt when that happened.

The rulers at that time considered themselves to be gods. The word had got out that a king was supposed to be born to a Jewish woman. King Herod feared this new king might replace him. To protect his kingdom he set out immediately to try to destroy any challenge to his kingship. Herod was motivated by Satan to destroy this infant Jesus Christ. Satan wanted to kill the worlds Savior so he could reign completely.

There is a lesson for us here; when we are fearful we are more susceptible to Satan's temptations than we would normally be. King Herod was driven to the point he commanded all male Jewish children under two years be killed. This killing of so many children was motivated by fear.

This quite birth in the town of Bethlehem had everlasting significance.

*6 The woman fled into the desert to a place prepared for her by God, where she might be taken care of for 1,260 days. (NIV)*

Some time later Herod died and Joseph was able to return to Israel but not Jerusalem. Instead Joseph set up a carpenter shop in Galilee where Jesus was raised.

Satan, the enormous red dragon, had a conflict with arch angel Michael and his angels. Michael overpowered Satan and threw him and his angels to the earth where they would not be accusing the residence of earth day and night. The stars that plunged to earth are considered to be Satan's angels. Hebrew traditions suggest one third of the angels in heaven fell to the earth with Satan.

Joseph took Mary to Egypt until it was safe for Jesus to return to the holy land. Because God aided Mary's escape we can be sure he offers security to all true believers. Satan attacks all believers; he may harm our physical bodies but God protects us from spiritual damage. We have Jesus' word that he will not lose one of these that God has given him. Jesus will not let Satan take the souls of God's true believers.

The 1,260 days, 42 months, 3 ½ years is the length of time that Mary was protected from the dragon. Three and one half is half of the perfect number seven. It falls far short of perfection which leaves incompleteness, imperfection, or even evil. Daniel predicted the holy city would be trampled by unbelievers for three and one half years (Daniel 12:7). The book of Revelation has numerous references to the number 3 1/2 years, 42 months, or 1260 days all meaning the same amount of time.

*7 And there was war in heaven. Michael and his angels fought against the dragon, and the dragon and his angels fought back. 8 But he was not strong enough, and they lost their place in heaven. (NIV)*

Remember Michael contented with Satan over Moses body. One of Michael's responsibilities is to guard God's community of believers. He stands ready to defend you at all times. Michael will see to it that everyone written in the Book of Life attends the final judgment. Only Christ's death and resurrection defeated the powers of evil. Christ's death on the cross has already defeated Satan and it is just a matter of time until Satan will be cast into the bottomless pit.

We have witnessed Satan's opposition to God in other parts of the Bible. However, this opposition causes Satan to be thrown out of heaven and onto the earth. Now Satan can no longer have frequent contact with God.

If you sometimes feel overpowered by your environment, remember even angels can be corrupted. Satan was a powerful angel of God. Satan became proud of his achievements and tried to assert his own will over the will of God. Satan constantly tries to hamper God's work and substitute his will in place of God's will. Satan is limited by God's power and can do only what God will allow (Job 1:6-2:8). Satan is the great accuser (12:10). Satan seeks out believers who are spiritually weak and who are isolated from other believers.

What was it that caused Satan to take such a bold opposition to God? Was it God's plan to send Jesus to earth to provide the sacrifice for the world's sins? Did this so infuriate Satan that it caused him to come into open conflict with God?

Even though God permits the devil to do his work in this world, God is still in control. And Jesus has complete power over Satan – he defeated Satan when he died and rose again for the sins of mankind. One day Satan will be bound forever, never again to do his evil work (20:10).

*9 The great dragon was hurled down-- that ancient serpent called the devil, or Satan, who leads the whole world astray. He was hurled to the earth, and his angels with him. 10 Then I heard a loud voice in heaven say: "Now have come the salvation and the power and the kingdom of our God, and the authority of his Christ. For the accuser of our brothers, who accuses them before our God day and night, has been hurled down. 11 They overcame him by the blood of the Lamb and by the word of their testimony; they did not love their lives so much as to shrink from death. (NIV)*

Here Satan's access to God is barred forever. Satan will not be able to accuse you of anything as long as he is here on earth. That does not mean he will not be able to tempt you to sin, he just will not be able to accuse you before God as he did with Job.

So, God's plan is set and there is no opposition to His plan. God has sent His son Jesus Christ to earth to be the sacrifice for mankind's sins. Can you fathom that kind of Love? Some of us send our sons off to services that may cost them their lives. However this is not just a chance of death, this is a plan that can only succeed if the death of Jesus Christ occurs.

As we face the battle with Satan we need not be fearful because Jesus Christ has already won the battle and triumphed over Satan. All we have to do is stay faithful in our beliefs about Jesus Christ being our Lord and Savor. Christ death paid the penalty for all our sins throughout all time. What greater love can one being have for another being than to give his life for all the people on earth through all time?

So why have a Satan at all? Why don't God just wipe him out and be done with it? How will you know your belief is true if it is not tested? We test most things we do, products we use, things we do, places we stay, and things we eat. Why should it be different with what we believe? Our faith grows stronger the more it is tested. Christ promised us that we would not be tested beyond our endurance. If you feel you are becoming overwhelmed pray for strength from God to meet your daily needs. We are living in the last days and Satan does not have much time to corrupt us and win us over to his side. He will try every trick available to have you join his followers. We need to stay close with our fellow believers to encourage each other and help each other through the difficult problems in life.

*12 Therefore rejoice you heavens and you who dwell in them! But woe to the earth and the sea, because the devil has gone down to you! He is filled with fury, because he knows that his time is short." 13 When the dragon saw that he had been hurled to the earth, he pursued the woman who had given birth to the male child. 14 The woman was given the two wings of a great eagle, so that she might fly to the place prepared for her in the desert, where she would be taken care of for a time, times and half a time, out of the serpent's reach. (NIV)*

Jesus escaped Satan's first attempt to kill Him; but, did Satan later succeed when he led the Jewish leadership to have Jesus crucified? I guess we will understand all of that when we see Jesus.

In case you do not recognize yourself we are her offspring's. Although Mary was Jewish all believers have been grafted into the Jewish blood line. You are in the bloodline of Jesus and joint heir with Jesus.

Apostle Paul tells us that we are in a spiritual battle (Ephesians 6:10-12). John tells us the war is still going on and our reading here in Revelation states they will be continuing until after we, the believers, have been harvested. Satan is looking for any weakness in our spiritual journey. Every time we grow angry Satan is waiting there to take advantage of it. Every time we become negative Satan is there to take advantage of any possible weakness. We are the prize Satan is struggling to convert, through our weakness, to his followers. Arm your spiritual commitment with the arch angel Michael's power and keep your heritage with Jesus Christ.

*15 Then from his mouth the serpent spewed water like a river, to overtake the woman and sweep her away with the torrent. 16 But the earth helped the woman by opening its mouth and swallowing the river that the dragon had spewed out of his mouth. 17 Then the dragon was enraged at the woman and went off to make war against the rest of her offspring-*

*- those who obey God's commandments and hold to the testimony of Jesus. (NIV)*

Did you get that direct hit? Satan's objective is to convert all Christians into his followers. With the powers of Satan our only possibility is the continual study of God's Word.

# REVELATION CHAPTER 13

*1 And the dragon stood on the shore of the sea. And I saw a beast coming out of the sea. He had ten horns and seven heads, with ten crowns on his horns, and on each head a blasphemous name. (NIV)*

As God has a messiah in Jesus Christ, so Satan will try to copy God and come up with a messiah. This beast coming out of the sea will be Satan's false messiah. This beast out of the sea (Satan's false messiah) is identified, by some, with the Roman Empire because of their encouragement of evil life-style, persecuting believers, and opposing God and His followers. Some say the beast is the Antichrist, not Satan but, someone under Satan's control.

We do know for sure the dragon (Satan) is in opposition to God. Satan and his angels have fought Michael and his angels. Satan was defeated and cast out of heaven and now resides on earth with all his angels. As we saw in chapter 12, when the Dragon swept a third of the stars from the sky, that is symbolic that Satan had converted one third of God's angels to his belief and they were cast to earth along with Satan.

*2 The beast I saw resembled a leopard, but had feet like those of a bear and a mouth like that of a lion. The dragon gave the beast his power and his throne and great authority. 3 One of the heads of the beast seemed to have had a fatal wound, but the fatal wound had been healed. The whole*

110

*world was astonished and followed the beast. (NIV)*

Some say that Daniel described this beast in his dream, take a look and see if you agree (Daniel 7). What do you think? Are Daniel and Revelation describing the same event? We do see many events in Revelation that seem to be taken from other parts of the Bible.

*4 Men worshiped the dragon because he had given authority to the beast, and they also worshiped the beast and asked, "Who is like the beast? Who can make war against him?" 5 The beast was given a mouth to utter proud words and blasphemies and to exercise his authority for forty-two months. 6 He opened his mouth to blaspheme God, and to slander his name and his dwelling place and those who live in heaven. 7 He was given power to make war against the saints and to conquer them. And he was given authority over every tribe, people, language and nation. 8 All inhabitants of the earth will worship the beast-- all whose names have not been written in the book of life belonging to the Lamb that was slain from the creation of the world. (NIV)*

Wow, it was looking bad there until verse 8 where all those in the book of life are not worshiping Satan and his false messiah. But, we are in for some more bad news. Where God is a (trinity) combination of three parts (Father, Son and

Holy Spirit) do you expect Satan to settle for less? No, we have another demon coming out of the earth.

*9 He who has an ear let him hear. 10 If anyone is to go into captivity, into captivity he will go. If anyone is to be killed with the sword, with the sword he will be killed. This calls for patient endurance and faithfulness on the part of the saints. (NIV)*

If you are a follower of Christ, have confessed your acceptance of Jesus Christ as your Lord and Savior, you are among the people called saints here. If you are in doubt of your sainthood check the book of James and be sure.

*11 Then I saw another beast, coming out of the earth. He had two horns like a lamb, but he spoke like a dragon. (NIV)*

Now Satan has completed the leadership part of his organization and is ready to start work in earnest. This trinity of Satan will learn by their failures and become more efficient in converting believers into non-believers as time goes on. You must remain strong in your faith to survive. The prime source for that strength is to continue the study of God's holy word in the Bible. Your choice is a personal one; this is not about the beliefs of any organization this is about your personal choice!

When Satan tempted Jesus in the desert, he wanted Jesus to show his power by turning stones into bread, to do miracles by jumping from a high place, and to gain political power by worshiping him (Matthew 4:1-11). Satan's plan was to rule the world through Jesus, but Jesus refused to do Satan's bidding. Thus Satan turns to the fearsome beasts described in

112

Revelation. To the beast out of the sea he gives political power. To the beast out of the earth he gives power to do miracles. Both beasts work together to capture the control of the whole world. This unholy trinity – the dragon, the beast out of the sea, and the false prophet (16:13) – unite in a desperate attempt to overthrow God, but their efforts are doomed to failure.

We see here that Satan even tempted our beloved Jesus. Do you think he will not tempt you? I think we have all experienced temptation and yes sometimes we fail. But we must always ask Christ to forgive our misdeeds and continue our struggle with even more strength. Eventually Satan will be destroyed and confined.

Have you ever noticed that when you really concentrate on something you are able to accomplish it? Well it is the same with Satan. Satan will give his complete concentration on conquering God's people and ruling over them. Satan will control the World economy and use that control to try to bring believers to his cause. Satan will desire for people to worship him and most will, everyone except the true believers. Be assured that Satan will not be able to harm you spiritually, only physically. The reward for refusing to follow the majority of people is the eternal life with God.

To be "dressed in white" means to be set apart for God and made pure. Christ promises future honor and eternal life to those who stand firm in their faith. The names of all believers are registered in the book of life. This book symbolizes God's knowledge of who belongs to him. All such people are guaranteed a listing in the book of life and are introduced to the host of heaven as belonging to Christ.

*12 He exercised all the authority of the first beast on his behalf, and made the earth and its inhabitants worship the first beast, whose fatal wound had been healed. 13 And he performed great and miraculous signs, even causing fire to come down from heaven to earth in full view of men. 14 Because of the signs he was given power to do on behalf of the first beast, he deceived the inhabitants of the earth. He ordered them to set up an image in honor of the beast that was wounded by the sword and yet lived. (NIV)*

God uses miracles as proof of his power, love, and authority. Here we see Satan creating fake miracles. These are deceptions designed to lead us away from Christ and his teachings. We read about Moses and Pharaoh's magicians and how they led Pharaoh into making decisions that were destructive to Egypt. If you read on you find out that Pharaoh's Calvary was drowned in the red sea leaving a much weakened Egypt.

How can you determine if a miracle is true or false? Every true miracle points to Jesus Christ, but miracles alone are deceptive. You must ask yourself, is this consistent with what is taught in the Bible?

*15 He was given power to give breath to the image of the first beast, so that it could speak and cause all who refused to worship the image to be killed. 16 He also forced everyone, small and great, rich and poor, free and slave, to receive a mark on his right hand or on his forehead, 17 so that no one could buy or sell unless he had the mark, which is the name of the beast or the number of his name. (NIV)*

In our occupations we are trained to accomplish the assignment we are given. If we do them diligently we receive rewards for the accomplishment. Yea, I know, sometimes it just means we get to keep our jobs. But generally a job well done has its rewards. So you are taught to cooperate with the system in charge. Even if you have a business of your own you must cooperate with other business people to accomplish your own goals. This makes us susceptible to accepting social norms. We need to examine these norms carefully and support what is good and healthy in our society. We must also oppose those things that are corrupt or harmful to our spiritual beings. We must do our best to avoid sin. Every sin that you tolerate gives Satan another way he can attack you.

*18 This calls for wisdom. If anyone has insight, let him calculate the number of the beast, for it is man's number. His number is 666. (NIV)*

We could get marred down in the mark of the beast and spend the rest of the study just discussing it. Let's not do that, the mark of the beast and God's mark come after the first crucifixion of the earth. We are still in the first six chapters of Revelation. We don't have to worry about the mark of the beast or God's mark. The way you live your life is proof enough that you are a Christian and are listed in the book of life. Do you remember in chapter 7 where the believers were marked by God?

# REVELATION CHAPTER 14

*1 Then I looked, and there before me was the Lamb, standing on Mount Zion, and with him 144,000 who had his name and his Father's name written on their foreheads. (NIV)*

Mount Zion is another name for Jerusalem. The war in heaven that caused Satan and his angels to be cast out of heaven and to earth started Satan's organization building in earnest. Satan had been successful with one third of the angels in heaven and they are still his loyal followers. Now Revelation is not chronological so we cannot be exactly sure when Satan arrived on earth. As much evil as we have on earth today could be interpreted that Satan is among us now. Some time between Job and now Satan has been cast to the Earth. What is your guess?

The 144,000 are the Jews that have kept their blood line pure according to the tribes of Israel. After the destruction of the earth and the intervention of God they have accepted Christ as their Lord and Savior. Their job is to bring the word of God to all the residence of earth. After these 144,000 have completed their work, bringing the word of God to the World, and there are no more conversions to Christ there must be another harvest of the believers.

After the seventh trumpet judgment the earth becomes the kingdom of our Lord and his Christ. You can expect some major changes on earth!

*2 And I heard a sound from heaven like the roar of rushing waters and like a loud peal of thunder. The sound I heard was like that of harpists playing their harps. 3 And they sang a new song before the throne and before the four living creatures and the elders. No one could learn the song except the 144,000 who had been redeemed from the earth. 4 These are those who did not defile themselves with women, for they kept themselves pure. They follow the Lamb wherever he goes. They were purchased from among men and offered as firstfruits to God and the Lamb. (NIV)*

Do you recognize Christ as the one with the voice like the roar of rushing waters? The loud peal of thunder usually means something significant is about to happen. These 144,000 have kept God and Christ in their conscious mind and obeyed his commands. They have converted non-believers to become believers for Christ. They have not adulterated their spiritual being with the practices of the pagan world around them.

*5 No lie was found in their mouths; they are blameless. 6 Then I saw another angel flying in midair, and he had the eternal gospel to proclaim to those who live on the earth-- to every nation, tribe, language and people. 7 He said in a loud voice, "Fear God and give him glory, because the hour of his judgment has come. Worship him who made the heavens, the earth, the sea and the springs of water." (NIV)*

After the seventh trumpet judgment an angel brings the word of God to all the nations. That does not release us of the responsibility to bring the word of God to all the nations of the world. It just states that after the trumpet judgments God's angel is going to make sure all hear God's truth. No one will have the excuse of not knowing God's word when the angel is finished. If you are reading this, you have already heard God's truth. You know that God's final judgment will not be put off forever. Have you joyfully received the everlasting Good News? Have you confessed your sins and trusted in Christ to save you? If so, you have nothing to fear from God's judgment. The Judge of all the earth is your Savior!

*8 A second angel followed and said, "Fallen! Fallen is Babylon the Great, which made all the nations drink the maddening wine of her adulteries." (NIV)*

Babylon invaded Judah, destroyed the temple, captured the leaders of Judah, and took the treasures of the temple back to Babylon (2 Kings 24 and 2 Chronicles 36). Babylon was the Jews worst enemy, as Rome was the early Christian worst enemy. John, already in exile on a remote island, could not speak of Rome directly without being killed. Using Babylon as the enemy of God's people allowed John to conceal his condemnation of Rome.

*9 A third angel followed them and said in a loud voice: "If anyone worships the beast and his image and receives his mark on the forehead or on the hand, 10 he, too, will drink of the wine of God's fury, which has been poured full strength into the cup of his wrath. He will be tormented with burning sulfur in the presence of the holy angels and of the Lamb. 11 And the smoke of their torment rises for ever and ever. There is no rest day or night for those who worship the beast and his image, or for anyone who receives the mark of his name." (NIV)*

This is after the seventh trumpet judgment and all God's people have His mark on their foreheads and Satan has marked all his followers with his mark on the forehead or right hand. The lines have been carefully drawn and the final battle is near. Even now our world values money, power and pleasure over spiritual concepts. Can you imagine what it will be like then? When you put your own wealth, power and pleasure above God's teachings you invite God's wrath (Psalm 75: Isaiah 51:17).

We were created in God's image. We have an inborn desire to fellowship with God. Sin cannot exist with God. When we sin we are separating ourselves from God. Recall the people that tried to follow Moses up the mountain when Moses was receiving the Ten Commandments? They were struck dead. When sin is allowed to continue it leads to death and permanent separation from God. If we allow sin to persist eternity with God will not be possible. If in this life we do not choose to be with God, in the next life we will be separated from God forever. Jesus invites us to open our hearts to Him and join Him in eternity with God.

*12 This calls for patient endurance on the part of the saints who obey God's commandments and remain faithful to Jesus. (NIV)*

Trust and obedience are the secret to remaining faithful to Jesus. We must trust in Jesus and continue to study God's word. We must search for the commands in his Word and obey them.

*13 Then I heard a voice from heaven say, "Write: Blessed are the dead who die in the Lord from now on." "Yes," says the Spirit, "they will rest from their labor, for their deeds will follow them." (NIV)*

Who says you can not take it with you? Well there are some things that you will take with you, your deeds, good and bad, follow you to eternity. Your deeds are recorded in the other book that is opened at our final judgment. Thank goodness that we have Jesus as our defense. Jesus has already paid the price for our sins, and as long as we are in the book of life, Jesus will be with us at our judgment.

*14 I looked, and there before me was a white cloud, and seated on the cloud was one "like a son of man" with a crown of gold on his head and a sharp sickle in his hand. 15 Then another angel came out of the temple and called in a loud voice to him who was sitting on the cloud, " Take your sickle and reap, because the time to reap has come, for the harvest of the earth is ripe." 16 So he who was seated on the cloud swung his sickle over the earth, and the earth was harvested. (NIV)*

Of course you recognize the son of man as Jesus Christ our Lord and Savior. Christ is separating the believers from the non-believers. If you are in the book of life you do not need to fear the Last Judgment (John 5:24).

*17 Another angel came out of the temple in heaven, and he too had a sharp sickle. 18 Still another angel, who had charge of the fire, came from the altar and called in a loud voice to him who had the sharp sickle, " Take your sharp sickle and gather the clusters of grapes from the earth's vine, because its grapes are ripe." 19 The angel swung his sickle on the earth, gathered its grapes and threw them into the great winepress of God's wrath. (NIV)*

A winepress is a large container where grapes are smashed. The juice is collected in a large holding container. The winepress is used as a symbol of God's anger and judgment in the Bible (Isaiah 63:3-6; Lamentations 1:15; Joel 3:12, 13).

Note here that there are two harvests of the believers on earth. We know one is when mankind first destroyed the earth and Jesus came to our rescue. It stands to reason the second one had to be after the 144,000 had completed their task and there were to be no more conversion to Christ.

*20 They were trampled in the winepress outside the city, and blood flowed out of the press, rising as high as the horses' bridles for a distance of 1,600 stadia. (NIV)*

A Greek stadium is 607 to 738 English feet. A Roman stadium is 606.95 English feet. If we use the Roman measure the 1600 stadia is 184 miles. If we use the Greek stadia the distance is 184 to 224 miles. However; the point here is not the exact length. The length here is about the north-south length of Palestine.

There is a lot of repetition in the Bible as witnessed by the four gospels where different people tell the story of Christ to different audiences. Each writer has his own version of what is important to their individual audiences. It is the same story just from a different view point.

Here in revelation we have verse 15 stating "Take your sickle and reap, because the time to reap has come, for the harvest of the earth is ripe." And then in verse 18 we see "Take your sharp sickle and gather the clusters of grapes from the earth's vine, because its grapes are ripe."

It is not common for the Bible to repeat like passages this close to each other. How we look at these two commands determine how we view the message of revelation. My personal belief is that these are two separate actions that take place at different times. We are living in an age where man has the ability to destroy the Earth. Before the Atomic age we were not capable of destroying the Earth. But, now we are, it only takes one carbon based atomic bomb to do permanent damage to the Earth. One carbon based atomic bomb, due to its fuel generating capability, could knock the Earth out of its orbit and cause the destruction of life on Earth as we know it.

The Jew/Arab hostilities could accelerate to the point where one irresponsible ruler could cause such a bomb to be built and detonated. Our support of Israel with continuing upgrading of their weapons by the United States could cause that kind of response from a single dictator.

The reference of the stars falling out of the sky could be the Earth going out of its normal orbit. A carbon bomb would definitely cause a huge crater with a large volume of smoke that would continue for years. In my story, God intervenes to prevent the destruction of all mankind and sets the Earth in a stable orbit. This is the harvest of believers referenced in verse 15.

After this there is no doubt that there is some superior force "God" that corrected man's folly and rescued the Earth. This demonstration of a superior force causes some to believe in Christ which requires the second harvest in verse 18. The rest of the populations of the Earth are in some other belief system that does not allow the belief in Jesus Christ our Lord and Savior. Please, do not take this as fact but form your own conclusion as to what these two verses mean.

# REVELATION CHAPTER 15

*1 I saw in heaven another great and marvelous sign: seven angels with the seven last plagues-- last, because with them God's wrath is completed. (NIV)*

We have entered the bowl judgments. The bowl judgments are total judgments, unlike the previous judgments. Where the seal judgments were for one fourth of the earth and the trumpet judgments were for one third of the earth. The bowl judgments will start in chapter 16 and will end with the destruction of all evil and the end of the world as we know it.

*2 And I saw what looked like a sea of glass mixed with fire and, standing beside the sea, those who had been victorious over the beast and his image and over the number of his name. They held harps given them by God (NIV)*

When we see a sea of glass, where are we (Revelation 4:6)? We are before the throne of God. The mixture of fire here represents the anger and judgment of God. Those standing beside the sea of glass are the people that persisted in their belief in Jesus Christ as our Lord and Savior.

*3 and sang the song of Moses the servant of God and the song of the Lamb: "Great and marvelous are your deeds, Lord God Almighty. Just and true are your ways, King of the ages. 4 Who will not fear you, O*

124

Lord, and bring glory to your name? For you alone are holy. All nations will come and worship before you, for your righteous acts have been revealed." (NIV)

The song of Moses celebrates Israel's escape from Egypt (Exodus 15), where the song of the Lamb celebrates our escape from the power of Satan.

5 After this I looked and in heaven the temple, that is, the tabernacle of the Testimony, was opened. 6 Out of the temple came the seven angels with the seven plagues. They were dressed in clean, shining linen and wore golden sashes around their chests. 7 Then one of the four living creatures gave to the seven angels seven golden bowls filled with the wrath of God, who lives for ever and ever. 8 And the temple was filled with smoke from the glory of God and from his power, and no one could enter the temple until the seven plagues of the seven angels were completed. (NIV)

The tabernacle of Testimony is the Greek translation for the Hebrew Tent of Meeting (Exodus 40:34, 35). Here one of the four living creatures gave the angels the bowls that contain God's anger. The angels here are dressed as high priest would be dressed. The angels clothing suggest they are free from corruption, immorality and injustice. The temple being filled with smoke represents God's glory and power. There is no escape from this judgment.

When the evil is destroyed by these judgments the eternal reign of Christ can begin. The faithful believers must wait for God's timetable.

# REVELATION CHAPTER 16

Before we start these final judgments let us review where we are and what is about to happen.

1. In chapter one; we were introduced to the risen Christ and His association with the Churches of all time.

2. In chapter two we received instruction from Christ about the conduct of churches in what is now Turkey.

3. In chapter three we received more instructions from Christ about the conduct of churches in what is now Turkey. These instructions included a list of things all churches should do and a list of things all churches should not do.

4. In chapter four we were introduced to God's throne room.

5. In chapter five we were reminded of why Christ is the only one qualified to open the seals to expose the future.

6. In chapter six we witnessed the opening of the seven seals. The earth was destroyed by man and restored by God.

7. We were introduced to the 144,000 Jews that converted to followers of Christ. All believers are marked by God. All Satan's followers are marked by Satan.

8. We witnessed the seven trumpet judgments. These judgments were directed to Satan's followers only.

9. We see Satan and his angels removed from heaven and thrown to earth.

10. The speech of the seven thunders is sealed to be told at a later time. John ate a small scroll which tasted sweet but turned his stomach sour.

11. We were introduced to the two witnesses that were killed and rose three days later.

12. In chapter twelve we see the dragon try to kill Christ at his birth.

13. In chapter thirteen we see the beast out of the sea and the beast out of land that form Satan's leadership team.

14. In chapter fourteen we see the 144,000 bringing the word of God to the nations. An angel brings the word of God for all people on earth to hear. We saw the harvest of the believers on earth.

15. In chapter fifteen we see the song of Moses and preparation for the final judgments.

16. In chapter sixteen we will see the bowl judgments. These are not partial judgments as the other judgments have been. These judgments are fully complete final judgments.

*1 Then I heard a loud voice from the temple saying to the seven angels, "Go, pour out the seven bowls of God's wrath on the earth." (NIV)*

The bowl judgments are God's final and complete judgments of the earth. These judgments are different from the seal and trumpet judgments. The seal judgments were limited to one quarter of the earth and people had opportunities to repent and choose to follow Christ. The trumpet judgments were limited to one third of the earth. Only the followers of Satan were subjected to the judgments. The indisputable evidence of a greater power exists. People were given the opportunity to repent and follow Christ. The bowl judgments are total judgments; there are no switching sides during these judgments. All people who have the mark of the beast on earth are directly involved in the bowl judgments.

*2 The first angel went and poured out his bowl on the land, and ugly and painful sores broke out on the people who had the mark of the beast and worshiped his image. 3 The second angel poured out his bowl on the sea, and it turned into blood like that of a dead man, and every living thing in the sea died. 4 The third angel poured out his bowl on the rivers and springs of water, and they became blood. 5 Then I heard the angel in charge of the waters say: "You are just in these judgments, you who are and who were, the Holy One, because you have so judged; 6 for they have shed the blood of your saints and prophets, and you have given them blood to drink as they deserve." 7 And I heard the altar respond: "Yes, Lord God Almighty, true and just are your judgments." (NIV)*

The altar's response signifies that everyone and everything will be praising God. All will understand His righteousness and justice. Notice also that only those that had the seal of the beast are subjected to the ugly and painful sores.

*8 The fourth angel poured out his bowl on the sun, and the sun was given power to* scorch people with fire. 9 They were seared by the intense heat and they cursed the name of God, who had control over these plagues, but they refused to repent and glorify him. 10 The fifth angel poured out his bowl on the throne of the beast, and his kingdom was plunged into darkness. Men gnawed their tongues in agony 11 and cursed the God of heaven because of their pains and their sores, but they refused to repent of what they had done. 12 The sixth angel poured out his bowl on the great river Euphrates, and its water was dried up to prepare the way for the kings from the East. (NIV)

In the midst of the pain and suffering all refused to repent of what they had been doing. Remember when Israel was crossing the Euphrates God held the waters back so the nation of Israel could cross the river. The Euphrates is a natural barrier that prevents empires from the east from entering the Promised Land. When the Euphrates is dried up the eastern nations have free access to all of the holy land. God previously has used the nations of the east to punish and scatter the Jews dwelling in the Promised Land.

13 Then I saw three evil spirits that looked like frogs; they came out of the mouth of the dragon, out of the mouth of the beast and out of the mouth of the false prophet. 14 They are spirits of demons performing miraculous signs, and they go out to the kings of the whole world, to gather them

*for the battle on the great day of God Almighty. (NIV)*

This is the start of Satan's and his angel's preparation to do battle with Christ and his angels. We have a good idea how this is going to turn out if we remember Satan's battle with Michael where Satan was defeated and he and his angels were thrown to earth. Note the characteristic of evil here; the nations were enticed to fight God by deceit and propaganda. They were not told about Satan's failure before in a similar battle. We see here that what you don't say is as important as what you do say.

These demons performing evil deeds were not created by Satan, God is the creator of all, and they are fallen angels that have joined Satan to tempt people to sin. Their main purpose on earth is to prevent, distort, or destroy people's relationship with God. While it is important to recognize their evil activities so we can stay away from them, we must avoid any curiosity about involvement with demonic forces or with the occult. Does that include fortune tellers? How about horoscopes?

*15 "Behold, I come like a thief! Blessed is he who stays awake and keeps his clothes with him, so that he may not go naked and be shamefully exposed." (NIV)*

No one, not even Christ, except the Father knows when the end will come. However; we see a hint here, when there is no more conversion to Christ the end is near (1 Thessalonians 5:1-6). We must prepare ourselves by continuing to study the word of God and continually improve our understanding of God's word. In what ways does your life show either your readiness, or your lack of preparation for Christ's return?

16 *Then they gathered the kings together to the place that in Hebrew is called Armageddon. (NIV)*

Armageddon is a battlefield southeast of the modern port of Haifa. The Armageddon battlefield is a large plain in northern Israel. There is a major highway leading from Egypt, through Israel, and on to Babylon. It is bounded southward by Galilee and westward by the mountains of Gilboa.

Does your personal battle with evil look like this battle pictured here? Do you stand for truth, peace, justice and morality? Are you ready to meet God and have all your evil removed? Be strong as you battle against sin and evil; you are fighting on the winning side.

17 *The seventh angel poured out his bowl into the air, and out of the temple came a loud voice from the throne, saying, "It is done!" 18 Then there came flashes of lightning, rumblings, peals of thunder and a severe earthquake. No earthquake like it has ever occurred since man has been on earth, so tremendous was the quake. 19 The great city split into three parts, and the cities of the nations collapsed. God remembered Babylon the Great and gave her the cup filled with the wine of the fury of his wrath. 20 Every island fled away and the mountains could not be found. 21 From the sky huge hailstones of about a hundred pounds each fell upon men. And they cursed God*

*on account of the plague of hail, because
the plague was so terrible. (NIV)*

The people here continue to curse God because they know
the judgments come from him; yet, they will not repent and
accept Christ. We should not be surprised by the hardness of
heart of the non-believer. We must reach out to the nonbeliever from where they are, not from where we are.
However; here it is too late to repent and follow Christ. All
of the people on earth are fully aware of God and they still
will not repent. Do you find yourself ignoring God in the
little things, like speeding? So do you need to turn back to
Christ before your heart is hardened to the point that you
cannot repent?

# REVELATION CHAPTER 17

*1 One of the seven angels who had the seven bowls came and said to me, "Come, I will show you the punishment of the great prostitute, who sits on many waters. (NIV)*

The "great prostitute" represents the early Roman Empire. It had many false gods and brutally martyred many Christians.

The many waters represent the well provisioned city of Rome. The prostitute represents the corrupt government and self serving officials who use immoral means to gain its own pleasure, prosperity and power. The wicked city of Babylon is opposite to the heavenly city of Jerusalem. John's followers identified Babylon with Rome, but Babylon could be any system that is hostile to God.

*2 With her the kings of the earth committed adultery and the inhabitants of the earth were intoxicated with the wine of her adulteries." 3 Then the angel carried me away in the Spirit into a desert. There I saw a woman sitting on a scarlet beast that was covered with blasphemous names and had seven heads and ten horns. (NIV)*

The influence of Rome was world wide in John's day. The red dragon is probably Satan or one of Satan's angels.

*4 The woman was dressed in purple and scarlet, and was glittering with gold,*

134

*precious stones and pearls. She held a golden cup in her hand, filled with abominable things and the filth of her adulteries. 5 This title was written on her forehead: MYSTERY BABYLON THE GREAT THE MOTHER OF PROSTITUTES AND OF THE ABOMINATIONS OF THE EARTH. 6 I saw that the woman was drunk with the blood of the saints, the blood of those who bore testimony to Jesus. When I saw her, I was greatly astonished. (NIV)*

Would you say she is gaudy? Does her attire show her feelings of triumph over the churches? Throughout history there have been people killed for their beliefs. Some were killed by oppressive governments, some by unregulated tribes and some even by street gangs. The woman's intoxication shows the pleasure she receives from her evil accomplishments. Do martyrs and challenges strengthen the faith of the church?

*7 Then the angel said to me: "Why are you astonished? I will explain to you the mystery of the woman and of the beast she rides, which has the seven heads and ten horns. 8 The beast, which you saw, once was, now is not, and will come up out of the Abyss and go to his destruction. The inhabitants of the earth whose names have not been written in the book of life from the creation of the world will be astonished when they see the beast, because he once was, now is not, and yet will come. (NIV)*

Once was, now is not, and yet will come must mean the thousand year period when the Dragon (Satan) is imprisoned. After the 1000 years he will be released again to test the faith of the believers. The return of the Dragons is similar to the persistence of evil. Evil returns stronger every time until it overpowers the person and leads to the second death.

*9 "This calls for a mind with wisdom. The seven heads are seven hills on which the woman sits. 10 They are also seven kings. Five have fallen, one is, the other has not yet come; but when he does come, he must remain for a little while. 11 The beast who once was, and now is not, is an eighth king. He belongs to the seven and is going to his destruction. (NIV)*

Rome was built on seven hills and this must be what John is referring to here. Some say, in John's day, Rome symbolized all evil in the world. Others say Rome symbolizes any person, religion, group, government or structure that opposes Christ. The point is that Satan is going to his destruction.

*12 "The ten horns you saw are ten kings who have not yet received a kingdom, but who for one hour will receive authority as kings along with the beast. (NIV)*

The ten horns represent the ten nations that will follow the fall of the Roman Empire. The Antichrist system will demand complete allegiance, rule with absolute power, oppression, and slavery. The ten kings will give their power to the Antichrist and will make war against the Lamb.

*13 They have one purpose and will give their power and authority to the beast. 14 They will make war against the Lamb, but the Lamb will overcome them because he is Lord of lords and King of kings-- and with him will be his called, chosen and faithful followers." 15 Then the angel said to me, "The waters you saw, where the prostitute sits, are peoples, multitudes, nations and languages. 16 The beast and the ten horns you saw will hate the prostitute. They will bring her to ruin and leave her naked; they will eat her flesh and burn her with fire. (NIV)*

Is that not the way evil works? The prostitute's friends turn on her and destroy her. Evil is destructive by its very nature. Evil leaves old friends when they are no longer useful. An evil organization is any troubled organization because each leader strives for his own interest.

*17 For God has put it into their hearts to accomplish his purpose by agreeing to give the beast their power to rule, until God's words are fulfilled. (NIV)*

Be sure that God is still in control and will overrule all plans of the evil one. God's plan will happen just as he says. God uses evil nations or people to accomplish his goals. God will eliminate all evil before he creates the new earth and new heaven.

*18 The woman you saw is the great city that rules over the kings of the earth."*
*(NIV)*

In John's day the Roman Empire ruled the known world.

# REVELATION CHAPTER 18

*1 After this I saw another angel coming down from heaven. He had great authority, and the earth was illuminated by his splendor. (NIV)*

This angel seems to be a dress rehearsal of the Christ's coming to earth. Not as widely seen as when Christ returns to earth but very impressive.

*2 With a mighty voice he shouted: "Fallen! Fallen is Babylon the Great! She has become a home for demons and a haunt for every evil spirit, a haunt for every unclean and detestable bird. 3 For all the nations have drunk the maddening wine of her adulteries. The kings of the earth committed adultery with her, and the merchants of the earth grew rich from her excessive luxuries." (NIV)*

John has used Babylon in different ways throughout Revelation; here, he is referring to everything that tries to block God's purpose will be demolished. This Babylon includes all the things in our affluent society that attract us away from Christ and God's work here on earth. Are you careful about how you spend your time? Life is so easily taken that we never know when we wake up in the morning if this will be our last day.

John, already in exile, did not dare write anything bad about Rome for fear of his life. John applied the name Babylon to the Jew's worst enemy (Roman Empire) and to all of God's enemy's of all time.

Merchants in the Roman Empire; and in fact today, grow prosperous by supplying the sinful desires of society. Businesses and Governments are, more and more, based on greed, money, and power. Are you wrapped up in the pursuit of money, status, and the good life? Do you live according to Christ's values; service, giving, self-sacrifice, obedience and truth?

*4 Then I heard another voice from heaven say: "Come out of her, my people, so that you will not share in her sins, so that you will not receive any of her plagues; 5 for her sins are piled up to heaven, and God has remembered her crimes. 6 Give back to her as she has given; pay her back double for what she has done. Mix her a double portion from her own cup. 7 Give her as much torture and grief as the glory and luxury she gave herself. In her heart she boasts, 'I sit as queen; I am not a widow, and I will never mourn.' 8 Therefore in one day her plagues will overtake her: death, mourning and famine. She will be consumed by fire, for mighty is the Lord God who judges her. (NIV)*

As compared to some other nations, we live in luxury and abundance. Does that give us a sense of being wealthy and powerful? Do you feel self assured, secure, and in control? Have you lost your feeling of need for God or anyone else? Do you defy God, will His punishment be harsh? Are you self-sufficient? Should gratitude be a large part of your life?

Should you use your resources to help others and advance God's work here on earth?

9 *"When the kings of the earth who committed adultery with her and shared her luxury see the smoke of her burning, they will weep and mourn over her. 10 Terrified at her torment, they will stand far off and cry: "'Woe! Woe, O great city, O Babylon, city of power! In one hour your doom has come!' (NIV)*

Many people have lost their retirement funds during the recent economic down turn. Lots of 401Ks have had drastic reduction in value and some no longer exist. Do you work only for material gains? If so you will have nothing when you die or when your possessions are destroyed. What can we take with us to the New Earth? Can you take your money, power or pleasure with you? No, but you will take your faith, deeds and your love of God; which are your true treasure.

11 *"The merchants of the earth will weep and mourn over her because no one buys their cargoes any more—12 cargoes of gold, silver, precious stones and pearls; fine linen, purple, silk and scarlet cloth; every sort of citron wood, and articles of every kind made of ivory, costly wood, bronze, iron and marble; 13 cargoes of cinnamon and spice, of incense, myrrh and frankincense; of wine and olive oil, of fine flour and wheat; cattle and sheep; horses and carriages; and bodies and souls of men. (NIV)*

141

Do you see any necessities of life in this list? Do they represent extreme materialism of our society? How about the bodies and souls or people? Have we become so self indulgent that people are willing to do anything in pursuit of our desired positions? Do some use evil means to satisfy their desires? Slaves are uncommon today however; are not prostitutes a form of slavery?

14 "They will say, 'The fruit you longed for is gone from you. All your riches and splendor have vanished, never to be recovered.' 15 The merchants who sold these things and gained their wealth from her will stand far off, terrified at her torment. They will weep and mourn 16 and cry out: "'Woe! Woe, O great city, dressed in fine linen, purple and scarlet, and glittering with gold, precious stones and pearls! 17 In one hour such great wealth has been brought to ruin!' "Every sea captain, and all who travel by ship, the sailors, and all who earn their living from the sea, will stand far off. 18 When they see the smoke of her burning, they will exclaim, 'Was there ever a city like this great city?' 19 They will throw dust on their heads, and with weeping and mourning cry out: "'Woe! Woe, O great city, where all who had ships on the sea became rich through her wealth! In one hour she has been brought to ruin! (NIV)

What would happen if the World economy were to collapse? Could we go back to an agrarian society? Have we grown so fat and lazy that we can no longer do the difficult work of tending the soil and harvesting crops? Are there too many people for us to go back to an agrarian society? Would many mourn the fall of the economy? How about governments? Would there be any taxes to support their elaborate spending? Would the transportation systems collapse? Will the fall of the world economy impact all that depend on it?

Will money be worthless in eternity? Will you be able to take any of your worldly possessions with you? The only things you can take to eternity are your beliefs, your acceptance or denial of Christ, and your deeds, both good and bad. Can we allow our lives to be dominated by greed?

*20 Rejoice over her, O heaven! Rejoice, saints and apostles and prophets! God has judged her for the way she treated you.'" 21 Then a mighty angel picked up a boulder the size of a large millstone and threw it into the sea, and said: "With such violence the great city of Babylon will be thrown down, never to be found again. 22 The music of harpists and musicians, flute players and trumpeters, will never be heard in you again. No workman of any trade will ever be found in you again. The sound of a millstone will never be heard in you again. 23 The light of a lamp will never shine in you again. The voice of bridegroom and bride will never be heard in you again. Your merchants were the world's great men. By your magic spell all the nations were led astray. 24 In her was found the blood of prophets and of the saints, and of all who have been killed on the earth." (NIV)*

The benefits of the world economy bring us tremendous enjoyment and comfort. Mixed with this comfort and enjoyment there is the requirement for some kind of action on our part. Some of these actions are beneficial to mankind and the earth. Some however; are destructive to our moral fiber and destructive to the earth.

# REVELATION CHAPTER 19

*1 After this I heard what sounded like the roar of a great multitude in heaven shouting: "Hallelujah! Salvation and glory and power belong to our God, (NIV)*

Who is your favorite sports athlete? Do you cheer when an outstanding performance is accomplished? Have you really considered what God has done for you? Can you get outside yourself enough to praise God for your very life? Have you recognized yourself as a sinful person dependent upon God for forgiveness? Have you praised him for forgiving all your sins? When you praise someone you are expressing your heart felt love for that person, praise God.

*2 for true and just are his judgments. He has condemned the great prostitute who corrupted the earth by her adulteries. He has avenged on her the blood of his servants." (NIV)*

The great prostitute here represents the Roman Empire and its corruption and the blood of many Christians. But; were they any worse than many of our existing governments? You probably do not know many Christians being killed just because they are Christians, but there are many other forms of corruption. Our governments work by accepting compromises to gain support from different thinking factions. Each faction maneuvers to gain pleasure, prosperity and advantage for itself.

*3 And again they shouted: "Hallelujah! The smoke from her goes up for ever and ever." 4 The twenty-four elders and the four living creatures fell down and worshiped God, who was seated on the throne. And they cried: "Amen, Hallelujah!" 5 Then a voice came from the throne, saying: "Praise our God, all you his servants, you who fear him, both small and great!" 6 Then I heard what sounded like a great multitude, like the roar of rushing waters and like loud peals of thunder, shouting: "Hallelujah! For our Lord God Almighty reigns. 7 Let us rejoice and be glad and give him glory! For the wedding of the Lamb has come, and his bride has made herself ready. 8 Fine linen, bright and clean, was given her to wear." (Fine linen stands for the righteous acts of the saints.) (NIV)*

All those in the Book of Life, saints, have gathered in praise of God for the destruction of evil. We are about to witness the wedding of the Lamp of God to the Christian church. However there is a step we have overlooked; somewhere during this process we have skipped over the process that removes all evil from us individually. We are not capable of removing sin from our nature and depend on Christ to purify us. This process apparently has happened because we are dressed in fine linen, bright, and clean which stands for the righteous acts of the saints Mathew 25:1-13).

This is the end of human history, the judgment of the wicked and the wedding of the Lamb of God to the Christian church.

146

The church includes all faithful believers of all time, those that existed during the seals judgment and the trumpet judgments. The saints clothing represents the righteousness of the saints instead of the gaudy attire of the great prostitute. The righteousness of the saints represents the work of Christ to save us from our sinful nature.

*9 Then the angel said to me, "Write: 'Blessed are those who are invited to the wedding supper of the Lamb!'" And he added, "These are the true words of God." 10 At this I fell at his feet to worship him. But he said to me, "Do not do it! I am a fellow servant with you and with your brothers who hold to the testimony of Jesus. Worship God! For the testimony of Jesus is the spirit of prophecy." (NIV)*

Wow, it would be easy to become overwhelmed in such a setting, and apparently John did when he fell down to worship this angel. "Worship only God! For the testimony of Jesus is the spirit of prophecy." Only God is worthy of your praise and worship. Jesus' redemptive plan is the central focus of God's revelation. As you study the book of Revelation, don't get caught up in all the details; remember that the real theme is the ultimate victory of Jesus Christ over all evil.

*11 I saw heaven standing open and there before me was a white horse, whose rider is called Faithful and True. With justice he judges and makes war. (NIV)*

Who is this "Faithful and True"? It is Jesus the source of all truth. This war will be the end of all wars.

147

**12** *His eyes are like blazing fire, and on his head are many crowns. He has a name written on him that no one knows but he himself. (NIV)*

Although Jesus calls himself by many names, as we read in chapters two and three, he is greater than any description the human mind can comprehend. There is no human name that can do Him justice.

**13** *He is dressed in a robe dipped in blood, and his name is the Word of God. (NIV)*

Jesus Christ is the greatest purifier because only He can remove the stain of sin. Sinlessness and holiness as represented by white and can only be given by Jesus Christ. This is how we are saved through faith (Isaiah 1:18; Romans 3:21-26).

**14** *The armies of heaven were following him, riding on white horses and dressed in fine linen, white and clean.* **15** *Out of his mouth comes a sharp sword with which to strike down the nations. "He will rule them with an iron scepter." He treads the winepress of the fury of the wrath of God Almighty.* **16** *On his robe and on his thigh he has this name written: KING OF KINGS AND LORD OF LORDS. (NIV)*

King of Kings and Lord of Lords show God's sovereignty. Now that the believers have been removed from the earth most of the world is worshiping Satan and his demons. Suddenly out of heaven comes the risen Christ in all his glory followed by his army. Christ's entrance announces the end of Satan's reign and start of the reign of the King of King and Lord of Lords. This is the end of false powers.

*17 And I saw an angel standing in the sun, who cried in a loud voice to all the birds flying in midair, "Come, gather together for the great supper of God, (NIV)*

This "great supper of God" is a grim view of what is about to happen to the followers of Satan and the beasts.

*18 so that you may eat the flesh of kings, generals, and mighty men, of horses and their riders, and the flesh of all people, free and slave, small and great." 19 Then I saw the beast and the kings of the earth and their armies gathered together to make war against the rider on the horse and his army. (NIV)*

Satan and his beasts have united the forces of earth to join in the battle against Christ and his army.

*20 But the beast was captured, and with him the false prophet who had performed the miraculous signs on his behalf. With these signs he had deluded those who had received the mark of the beast and worshiped his image. The two of them were thrown alive into the fiery lake of burning sulfur. (NIV)*

The beast and the false prophet were thrown into the lake of burning sulfur, which is the final resting place for the wicked.

*21 The rest of them were killed with the sword that came out of the mouth of the rider on the horse, and all the birds gorged themselves on their flesh. (NIV)*

The greatest war in the history of the world is about to begin. The Antichrist and the false prophet have gathered the governments and armies of the earth under the Antichrist's rule. God has summoned them to battle in order to defeat them. Their pride and rebellion have perverted their thinking. There really is no fight, however, because the victory was won when Jesus died on the cross for sin and rose from the dead. The evil leaders are immediately captured and sent to the lake of burning sulfur.

# REVELATION CHAPTER 20

*1 And I saw an angel coming down out of heaven, having the key to the Abyss and holding in his hand a great chain. (NIV)*

The key to the Abyss (bottomless pit) is normally held by Christ. But Christ is leading the battle against all evil, and is a little busy at this time. This angel here must have been given the key temporarily; however this angel is under God's control and authority. The Abyss is the destination of Satan and his demons.

*2 He seized the dragon, that ancient serpent, who is the devil, or Satan, and bound him for a thousand years. (NIV)*

Satan is not bound for punishment here, but to prevent him from deceiving the nations.

*3 He threw him into the Abyss, and locked and sealed it over him, to keep him from deceiving the nations anymore until the thousand years were ended. After that, he must be set free for a short time. (NIV)*

After 1000 years Satan will be released to test the faith of the believers. Satan's release will result in the final destruction of all evil. People that claim their belief in Christ will be tested by temptation as we are today.

*4 I saw thrones on which were seated those who had been given authority to judge.*

151

*And I saw the souls of those who had been beheaded because of their testimony for Jesus and because of the word of God. They had not worshiped the beast or his image and had not received his mark on their foreheads or their hands. They came to life and reigned with Christ a thousand years. (NIV)*

Revelation is not chronological and; therefore, it is hard to determine when these 1000 years will happen. I feel it will not be until the seal judgments are completed which means none of us will be there. There will be nothing during these 1000 years to tempt us so it certainly is not now, we have abundant temptation. Scholars have made as big a deal of this period as they did the number 666, neither of which relates to us during the seals judgments.

*5 (The rest of the dead did not come to life until the thousand years were ended.) This is the first resurrection. 6 Blessed and holy are those who have part in the first resurrection. The second death has no power over them, but they will be priests of God and of Christ and will reign with him for a thousand years. (NIV)*

This will be 1000 years where Christ is in firm control of all nations of the world. There will be no war as our Lord and Savior reigns.

*7 When the thousand years are over, Satan will be released from his prison 8 and will go out to deceive the nations in the four*

152

*corners of the earth-- Gog and Magog-- to gather them for battle. In number they are like the sand on the seashore. 9 They marched across the breadth of the earth and surrounded the camp of God's people, the city he loves. But fire came down from heaven and devoured them. (NIV)*

It should be noted here the battle is not fought with believers but God himself rains down fire from heaven to destroy them. There is no doubt about how this battle is going to turn out. The fire from heaven devours Satan and his attacking armies. If you are with God you will see the victory with Christ.

*10 And the devil, who deceived them, was thrown into the lake of burning sulfur, where the beast and the false prophet had been thrown. They will be tormented day and night for ever and ever. (NIV)*

For the 1000 years Satan was confined in the bottomless pit here he is thrown into the lake of burning sulfur where the beast and false prophet were thrown. Satan was released from the bottomless pit but he will never be released from the lake of burning sulfur. Satan will never tempt anyone ever again.

*11 Then I saw a great white throne and him who was seated on it. Earth and sky fled from his presence, and there was no place for them. 12 And I saw the dead, great and small, standing before the throne, and books were opened. Another book was opened, which is the book of life. The dead were judged according to what they had done as recorded in the books. 13 The sea gave up the dead that were in it, and death and Hades gave up the dead that were in them, and each person was judged according to what he had done. 14 Then death and Hades were thrown into the lake of fire. The lake of fire is the second death. (NIV)*

This is the final individual judgment it is not just the book of life, where you chose to follow Jesus Christ, but also a book of your deeds while you were here on earth. Yes, how you lived your life will be reviewed. All those things you wish you had not done will be brought up and discussed again. However; this time there will be no escaping the truth, but you will have Jesus Christ as your defense attorney and he has already paid for all your sins.

*15 If anyone's name was not found written in the book of life, he was thrown into the lake of fire. (NIV)*

The Book of Life documents your selection of Jesus Christ as your Lord and Savior. If your name is not in this book you are thrown into the lake of fire.

# REVELATION CHAPTER 21

*1 Then I saw a new heaven and a new earth, for the first heaven and the first earth had passed away, and there was no longer any sea. (NIV)*

After God's judgments are complete God will create a new earth (Romans 8:18-21; 2 Peter 3:7-13). God promised Isaiah that he would create a new and eternal earth (Isaiah 65:17; 66:22). We are not told where the new earth will be but God will be with us on the earth. There will be no need for the sun, moon, planets, stars, or even galaxies. God and his followers, those written in the book of life, will be there.

*2 I saw the Holy City, the New Jerusalem, coming down out of heaven from God, prepared as a bride beautifully dressed for her husband. 3 And I heard a loud voice from the throne saying, "Now the dwelling of God is with men, and he will live with them. They will be his people, and God himself will be with them and be their God. (NIV)*

Finally we will have the realization of God with man. What a glorious future is ahead of us. Where God reigns there is only peace, security, and love.

*4 He will wipe every tear from their eyes. There will be no more death or mourning*

155

or crying or pain, for the old order of things has passed away." (NIV)

If we are going to be there for eternity then we must not grow old, or at least deteriorate with age as we do now. And if we are to be there for eternity then things must not deteriorate, we don't have to worry about replacing the appliances every few years. The New Jerusalem will be beyond our present comprehension, it will far exceed our fondest expectations.

5 He who was seated on the throne said, "I am making everything new!" Then he said, "Write this down, for these words are trustworthy and true." (NIV)

God is the creator of all things! The Bible starts with the creating of the universe and ends with the creation of a New Heaven and New Earth. When we see Jesus, with our sins forgiven, we will be made perfect like Him, and reside with God through eternity. Making everything new here is not like buying a new house where it grows old with time, needs repair and eventually needs replacement. The new here is forever!

6 He said to me: "It is done. I am the Alpha and the Omega, the Beginning and the End. To him who is thirsty I will give to drink without cost from the spring of the water of life. (NIV)

God finished the work of creation (Genesis 2:1-3), and Jesus finished the work of redemption (John 19:30), so the Trinity will finish the plan of salvation by collecting all that are listed in the Book of Life.

*7 He who overcomes will inherit all this, and I will be his God and he will be my son. 8 But the cowardly, the unbelieving, the vile, the murderers, the sexually immoral, those who practice magic arts, the idolaters and all liars-- their place will be in the fiery lake of burning sulfur. This is the second death." (NIV)*

Doubting your faith is not what we are talking about, we are talking about turning back from following God. One must be brave enough to stand up for Christ and humble enough to accept God's authority over you.

People who stand firm to the end will receive the blessings that God promised:

* 1 Eating from the tree of life 2:7,

* 2 Escaping from the lake of fire (the "second death," ) 2:11,

* 3 Receiving a special name 2:17,

* 4 Having authority over the nations 2:26,

* 5 Being included in the book of life 3:5,

* 6 Being a pillar in God's spiritual temple 3:12, and

* 7 Sitting with Christ on his throne 3:21.

Those who are tested and proven to remain faithful will be rewarded by God.

**Revelation 2:7 He who has an ear let him hear what the Spirit says to the churches. To him who overcomes, I will give the right to eat from the tree of life, which is in the paradise of God. (NIV)**

Revelation 2:11 He who has an ear let him hear what the Spirit says to the churches. He who overcomes will not be hurt at all by the second death. (NIV)

Revelation 2:17 He who has an ear let him hear what the Spirit says to the churches. To him who overcomes, I will give some of the hidden manna. I will also give him a white stone with a new name written on it, known only to him who receives it. (NIV)

Revelation 2:26 To him who overcomes and does my will to the end, I will give authority over the nations-- (NIV)

Revelation 3:5 He who overcomes will, like them, be dressed in white. I will never blot out his name from the book of life, but will acknowledge his name before my Father and his angels. (NIV)

Revelation 3:12 Him who overcomes I will make a pillar in the temple of my God. Never again will he leave it. I will write on him the name of my God and the name of the city of my God, the new Jerusalem, which is coming down out of heaven from my God; and I will also write on him my new name. (NIV)

Revelation 3:21 To him who overcomes, I will give the right to sit with me on my throne, just as I overcame and sat down with my Father on his throne. (NIV)

9 One of the seven angels who had the seven bowls full of the seven last plagues came and said to me, "Come, I will show you the bride, the wife of the Lamb." 10 And he carried me away in the Spirit to a mountain great and high, and showed me the Holy City, Jerusalem, coming down out of heaven from God. (NIV)

So, John saw the indescribable City of God, the New Jerusalem must have been an awesome sight.

*11 It shone with the glory of God, and its brilliance was like that of a very precious jewel, like jasper, clear as crystal. 12 It had a great, high wall with twelve gates and with twelve angels at the gates. On the gates were written the names of the twelve tribes of Israel. 13 There were three gates on the east, three on the north, three on the south and three on the west. 14 The wall of the city had twelve foundations, and on them were the names of the twelve apostles of the Lamb. (NIV)*

God's future home sounds very beautiful, with a high wall all around it and three gates on each of the four sides. All the faithful in the Old Testament are represented by the twelve gates and the faithful of the New Testament (the church) are represented by the foundations of the wall. All races will live together in the New Jerusalem.

*15 The angel who talked with me had a measuring rod of gold to measure the city, its gates and its walls. 16 The city was laid out like a square, as long as it was wide. He measured the city with the rod and found it to be 12,000 stadia in length, and as wide and high as it is long. 17 He measured its wall and it was 144 cubits thick, by man's measurement, which the angel was using. (NIV)*

A cubit is the length of the forearm from the elbow to the tip of the middle finger. The cubit is generally accepted to be 18 to 21 inches long. The wall width of 144 cubits would be from 216 feet to 252 feet thick according to which measure (18 to 21 inches) you use. We are not told how high the great high wall is, only how thick. However, entry into the New Jerusalem is through one of the 12 gates so it must be a pretty high wall to allow all traffic to and from all the nations of the New Earth.

The city was laid out like a square, but was as high as it was on each side. This city then is a cube of 12,000 stadia for each side and height. The Greek measure for a stadium is from 607 English feet to 738 English feet. The Roman stadium is 606.95 English feet. If we use the Roman measure the 12,000 stadia would be 1379 miles cube. If you tried to put that size of a city on our earth it would sink, throw the earth out of balance, and probably send it whirling out into space. So, this earth that receives the New Jerusalem is a much larger place than the earth we know today. With God being with us we do not need the universe. Did God use all the material in the universe to create the New Earth and New Jerusalem? The New Jerusalem was the same shape as in the inner sanctuary in the old Testament (1 King 6:20).

**I King 6:20 The inner sanctuary was twenty cubits long, twenty wide and twenty high. He overlaid the inside with pure gold, and he also overlaid the altar of cedar. (NIV)**

The inner sanctuary is not a small structure either. Twenty cubits is between 30 and 35 cubic feet.

*18 The wall was made of jasper, and the city of pure gold, as pure as glass. 19 The foundations of the city walls were decorated with every kind of precious stone. The first foundation was jasper, the second sapphire, the third chalcedony, the fourth emerald, 20 the fifth sardonyx, the sixth carnelian, the seventh chrysolite, the eighth beryl, the ninth topaz, the tenth chrysoprase, the eleventh jacinth, and the twelfth amethyst. 21 The twelve gates were twelve pearls, each gate made of a single pearl. The great street of the city was of pure gold, like transparent glass. (NIV)*

The wall made of Jasper would be opaque cryptocrystalline quartz of any of several colors; green chalcedony, or blackish green.

The first foundation for the wall will be made form Jasper the same material as the wall itself is composed of.

The second foundation for the wall is made of Sapphire; a gem variety of corundum in transparent or translucent crystals of color other than red, transparent rich blue or a variable color averaging a deep purplish blue.

The third foundation of the wall is made of Chalcedony; a translucent quartz that is commonly pale blue or gray with nearly wax like luster.

The fourth foundation of the wall is made of Emerald; a rich green variety of beryl prized as a gemstone, and brightly or richly green.

The fifth foundation of the wall is made of Sardonyx; an onyx having parallel layers of sard. Sard is a deep orange-red variety of chalcedony classed by some as a variety of carnelian and Onyx is a translucent chalcedony in parallel layers of different colors.

The sixth foundation of the wall is made of Carnelian; a hard tough chalcedony that has a reddish color and is used in jewelry.

The seventh foundation of the wall is made of Chrysolite; a mineral consisting of a fibrous silky serpentine and constituting a kind of asbestos.

The eight foundation of the wall is made of Beryl, a mineral consisting of a silicate of beryllium and aluminum of great hardness and occurring in green, bluish green, yellow, pink, or white hexagonal prisms.

The ninth foundation of the wall is made of Topaz; essentially a silicate of aluminum and usually occurs in orthorhombic translucent or transparent crystals or in white translucent masses, yellow to brownish yellow transparent mineral topaz used as a gem, yellow sapphire, or yellow quartz.

The tenth foundation of the wall is made of Chrysoprase: an apple-green chalcedony valued as a gem.

The eleventh foundation of the wall is made of Jacinth; a gem more nearly orange in color than a hyacinth.

The twelfth foundation of the wall is made of Amethyst; clear purple or bluish violet variety of crystallized quartz, a deep purple variety of corundum, or a variable color averaging a moderate purple.

Wow, with just a wall like that what must the building look like?

*22 I did not see a temple in the city, because the Lord God Almighty and the Lamb are its temple. 23 The city does not need the sun or the moon to shine on it, for the glory of God gives it light, and the Lamb is its lamp. 24 The nations will walk by its light, and the kings of the earth will bring their splendor into it. (NIV)*

Jesus told us that where two or more were gathered in his name he would be there. So our churches or temples are our primary place of worship. In the New Jerusalem God's presence will be everywhere and there will be no need for a temple. God will be worshiped throughout the city and nothing will separate us from Him.

*25 On no day will its gates ever be shut, for there will be no night there. 26 The glory and honor of the nations will be brought into it. 27 Nothing impure will ever enter it, nor will anyone who does what is shameful or deceitful, but only those whose names are written in the Lamb's book of life. (NIV)*

There is one list you must make if you desire to live in the New Jerusalem; that is the Lamb's book of life (your acceptance of Jesus Christ as your Lord and Savior). Your good deeds, status here on earth, background, personality, or good behavior will not get you into the New Jerusalem. It is not about what you do, it is about what Jesus has already done for you. Give your life to Jesus today so you may join the saints in the New Jerusalem.

Its like, God takes notes, and list all who accept Jesus Christ as their Lord and Savior. This list is the only list that will get you an invitation to join God in the New Jerusalem. The acceptance of Jesus Christ is your recognition that you are not capable of living the sinless life and need divine forgiveness for all your sins.

163

# REVELATION CHAPTER 22

*1 Then the angel showed me the river of the water of life, as clear as crystal, flowing from the throne of God and of the Lamb (NIV)*

Do you remember Jesus talking to the Samaritan woman (John 4:7-14)? Believing in Jesus will satisfy our spiritual thirst for all eternity.

*2 down the middle of the great street of the city. On each side of the river stood the tree of life, bearing twelve crops of fruit, yielding its fruit every month. And the leaves of the tree are for the healing of the nations. (NIV)*

Remember the Garden of Eden (Genesis 2:9) and its tree of life? Well now we will be able to eat from the tree of life and live forever. There will be no sin or evil in the New Jerusalem. The fruit of the month will add variety to our pleasure. The leaves of the tree of life will be used to heal the nations.

John is referring to Ezekiel 47:12 where the trees with the healing leaves are revealed.

**Ezekiel 47:12 Fruit trees of all kinds will grow on both banks of the river. Their leaves will not wither, nor will their fruit fail. Every month they will bear, because the water from the sanctuary flows to them. Their fruit will serve for food and their leaves for healing." (NIV)**

164

From this it looks like we will still eat and if there is sickness in the nations we will have a ready cure for all ailments.

*3 No longer will there be any curse. The throne of God and of the Lamb will be in the city, and his servants will serve him. (NIV)*

We can throw away all the weeding tools and just enjoy the blooms and fruit of the plants. "No longer will there be any curse" means that we will be secure in God's presence (Zechariah 14:11).

*4 They will see his face, and his name will be on their foreheads. 5 There will be no more night. They will not need the light of a lamp or the light of the sun, for the Lord God will give them light. And they will reign for ever and ever. 6 The angel said to me, "These words are trustworthy and true. The Lord, the God of the spirits of the prophets, sent his angel to show his servants the things that must soon take place." 7 "Behold, I am coming soon! Blessed is he who keeps the words of the prophecy in this book." 8 I, John, am the one who heard and saw these things. And when I had heard and seen them, I fell down to worship at the feet of the angel who had been showing them to me. 9 But he said to me, "Do not do it! I am a fellow servant with you and with your brothers the prophets and of all who keep the words of this book. Worship God!" (NIV)*

John's report on what he witnessed in Revelation is the next best thing to directly witnessing the events of Revelation. John wrote down all he could comprehend so we could believe and be saved from the lake of burning sulfur. You have read this far, have you believed? John's last instruction was to Worship God, let us continue that worship!

We, as a people of God, are becoming more aware of the capability of our mind. This awesome gift from God has potential that we are just now starting to be understood, yet we only use less than 10% of our mental capability. When we see Jesus and become purified we will be capable of being obedient to God's command to "Love the Lord your God with all your heart and with all your soul and with your entire mind (Matthew 22:37)." Are there people, ideas, goals, or possessions that occupy the dominate place in your mind, crowding God out? Worship only God by allowing nothing to distract you from your devotion to him.

**Matthew 22:37 Jesus replied: "'Love the Lord your God with all your heart and with all your soul and with all your mind.' (NIV)**

*10 Then he told me, "Do not seal up the words of the prophecy of this book, because the time is near. 11 Let him who does wrong continue to do wrong; let him who is vile continue to be vile; let him who does right continue to do right; and let him who is holy continue to be holy." (NIV)*

Here John has received instruction to not seal up the words of prophecy but allow us to read and understand what is written in Revelation. It is time to set aside the fear associated with the study of Revelation and start using its directions to enhance our belief in God the creator of our very lives and our universe. Unlike Daniel's prophecy John's prophecy is to be read and understood; it was relevant in John's time and it is relevant to our time today. Satan's followers are learning every day and are dedicated to the one purpose of leading believers into temptations that destroy our faith and separate us from God.

*12 "Behold, I am coming soon! My reward is with me, and I will give to everyone according to what he has done. 13 I am the Alpha and the Omega, the First and the Last, the Beginning and the End. 14 "Blessed are those who wash their robes, that they may have the right to the tree of life and may go through the gates into the city. (NIV)*

Only those that accept Jesus Christ's as their Savior can have their sins purified so they can enter into the New Jerusalem. Remember that sin and God cannot exist together. To be with God you must have your sins purified by the blood of Jesus Christ. We must strive to remain faithful until our death or until Christ returns. If we are faithful and remain faithful we will receive God's rewards.

There are many opinions about the Great Tribulation. Some believe it refers to the suffering of believers through all time. Others believe it refers to a specific time of intense tribulation yet to come. Others believe the Roman Empire was the great tribulation. I might as well add my thoughts to the collection. I believe we witnessed a great tribulation during the Roman Empire rule of the known world; but, I believe we will still see random occasions of tribulation throughout the seals judgments. During the trumpet judgments there will be great tribulations for believers and then there will also be the judgments that will be directed at the people that bear the sign of Satan and his angels. However, all of that is just speculation with no real goal. The concept here is that if you persist and remain faithful to God for the short period you live; you will receive God's reward and spend eternity with God in the New World and New Jerusalem.

*15 Outside are the dogs, those who practice magic arts, the sexually immoral, the murderers, the idolaters and everyone who loves and practices falsehood. (NIV)*

Where are these people? Are they thrown into the lake of burning sulfur? Nothing evil will ever enter the New Jerusalem and be in God's presence or harm any of God's faithful followers.

*16 "I, Jesus, have sent my angel to give you this testimony for the churches. I am the Root and the Offspring of David, and the bright Morning Star." (NIV)*

As the Word that created the universe Jesus was here long before there was any thought of King David. When "God" Jesus took on complete and total human form he was an offspring of David, that is a direct descendant of David (Isaiah 11:1-5; Matthew 1:1-17). As our Lord and Savior Jesus is our "Bright Morning Star" the light of salvation to all who will believe.

*17 The Spirit and the bride say, "Come!" And let him who hears say, "Come!" Whoever is thirsty, let him come; and whoever wishes, let him take the free gift of the water of life. (NIV)*

Both the Holy Spirit and the Church invite the entire world to come to Jesus and receive salvation in Christ. Christ invites everyone to come and drink the water of life; all people everywhere are invited to come! Salvation is not about what we do for Christ it is about what Christ has already done for all of us. Let us invite everyone!

*18 I warn everyone who hears the words of the prophecy of this book: If anyone adds anything to them, God will add to him the plagues described in this book. 19 And if anyone takes words away from this book of prophecy, God will take away from him his share in the tree of life and in the holy city, which are described in this book. (NIV)*

This warning has inhibited many students of Revelation and has unfortunately tended to vial or limit the study of Revelation. The intense Love of God for all people of earth cannot be found any other place more plainly than in Revelation. Our loving "God" father goes to extreme limits to show his love for us and almost begs us to accept his love. How can we be so hard-hearted to ignore his calling?

The purpose of the warning is to prevent the misuse of the Holy Word of God. How many times have you heard parts of the Bible being used to win an argument? Well, that is not the purpose of the Bible. The bible should be used to win souls for God through the cleansing blood of Jesus Christ so they can exist in the company of God. We must use the Bible with great respect so that we do not distort its meaning even unintentionally. Only the Holy Work of God is true and trustworthy, all other is mere human impressions of what is meant.

*20 He who testifies to these things says, "Yes, I am coming soon." Amen. Come, Lord Jesus. (NIV)*

As Jesus told us only the Father knows when the end of the world will come, however, we hear daily about the sudden and unexpected death of individuals. When your time comes will you be ready? I pray that you will be found faithful and true.

*21 The grace of the Lord Jesus be with God's people. Amen. (NIV)*

Revelation closed human history in the paradise of New Jerusalem, as Genesis opened human history in the Garden of Eden another paradise. Genesis tells of a direct relationship between God and human. Adam and Eve destroyed that relationship by disobeying God's command. Will we have the ability to obey God's commands enough to accept Christ's redemption and join God in the New Jerusalem? Paradise is recreated in the New Jerusalem.

The book of Revelation ends with an urgent request: "Come Lord Jesus." In a world of problems, persecution, evil, and immorality, Christ calls us to endure in our faith. Our efforts to better our world are important, but their results cannot compare with the transformation that Jesus will bring about when he returns. He alone controls human history, forgives sin, and will re-create the earth and bring lasting peace.

Revelation is, above all, a book of hope. It shows that no matter what happens on earth, God is in control. It promises that evil will not last forever. And it depicts the wonderful reward that is waiting for all those who believe in Jesus Christ as Lord and Savior.

# Summary of Explore Revelation

What did you learn from Explore Revelation? The first few times you read Revelation it is hard to comprehend what you are reading. After many readings Revelation becomes clearer and you start to understand what God is saying to each of us. Let us review what Revelation is saying to us.

**Chapter 1** starts by explaining how Revelation came into existence. Revelation is the word of God and the testimony of Jesus Christ. The blessing that comes with Revelation (1:3) is unique in the Bible. "Blessed is the one who reads the words of this prophecy, and blessed are those who hear it and take to heart what is written in it,…"

God the father, Jesus Christ the son, and the Holy Spirit are introduced and the many names addressed to each starts to unfold. The majesty of the risen Jesus Christ is described and Christ's relation with the Church is established. The mystery of the seven lamp stands and the seven stars is revealed.

Chapters 2 and 3 are Christ's instruction to the churches in what is now Turkey. These are Churches that knew John and his teachings. These instructions stand today as a guide for the operation of every church regardless of denomination.

## Names of Jesus Christ

These are the words of him who holds the seven stars in his right hand and walks among the seven golden lamp stands.

These are the words of him who is the First and the Last, who died and came to life again.

These are the words of him who has the sharp, double-edged sword.

171

These are the words of the Son of God, whose eyes are like blazing fire and whose feet are like burnished bronze.

These are the words of him who holds the seven spirits of God and the seven stars.

These are the words of him who is holy and true, who holds the key of David. What he opens no one can shut, and what he shuts no one can open.

These are the words of the Amen, the faithful and true witness, the ruler of God's creation.

## Praises

Hard work,

Perseverance,

Cannot tolerate wicked men,

You have tested apostles and found them false,

Endured hardship for my name,

Have not grown weary,

You hate the practices of the Nicolaitans,

I know your afflictions and your poverty - yet you are rich,

You remain true to my name,

You did not renounce your faith in me, even in the days of Antipas, my faithful witness who was put to death in your city – where Satan lives,

I know your love and faith,

I know your service and perseverance,

You are now doing more than you did at first, and

I know that you have little strength, yet you have kept my work and have not denied my name.

# Instructions

I hold this against you:

You have forsaken your first love,

Remember the height from which you have fallen,

Repent and do the things you did at first,

You have people there who hold to the teaching of Balaam, who taught Balak to entice the Israelites to sin by eating food sacrificed to idols and by committing sexual immorality,

You have those who hold to the teaching of the Nicolaitans,

You tolerate that woman Jezebel, who calls herself a prophetess,

Wake up, Strengthen what remains and is about to die,

I have not found your deeds complete in the sight of my God,

Remember what you have received and heard; obey it, and repent,

Hold on to what you have, so that no one will take your crown,

I counsel you to buy from me gold refined in the fire, so you can become rich; and white clothes to wear, so you can cover your shameful nakedness; and salve to put on your eyes , so you can see, and

Be earnest, and repent.


# Warning

If you do not repent:

I will come to you and remove your lamp stand from its place,

The devil will put some of you in prison to test you,

You will suffer persecution for ten days,

I will cast her on a bed of suffering,

I will make those who commit adultery with her suffer intensely,

I will strike her children dead,

I will repay each of you according to your deeds,

If you do not wake up, I will come like a thief, and you will not know at what time I will come to you, and

Because you are lukewarm - neither hot nor cold - I am about to spit you out of my mouth.

## Reward

To him who overcomes:

I will give the right to eat from the tree of life,

Be faithful, even to the point of death, and I will give you the crown of life,

To him who overcomes, I will give some of the hidden manna,

I will also give him a white stone with a new name written on it,

To him who overcomes and does my will to the end, I will give authority over the nations,

I will also give him the morning star,

Those who have not soiled their clothes will walk with me,

He who overcomes will be dressed in white,

I will never blot out his name from the book of life,

I will acknowledge his name before my Father and his angels,

For he who overcomes I will make a pillar in the temple of my God,

I will write on him the name of my God and the name of the city of my God, the new Jerusalem, which is coming down out of heaven from my God; and I will also write on him my new name,

If any one hears my voice and opens the door, I will come in and eat with him and he with me,

To him who overcome, I will give the right to sit with me on my throne, just as I overcome and sat down with my Father on his throne.

Consider the details Christ reveals about the churches, down to the activities of individuals. Do you believe Christ knows about your church? Does Christ know you are a member? Are you in His Book of Life? Does that assure you a place in the New Jerusalem?

**Chapter 4 and 5** gives us our first look at God's throne and the thrones of the 24 elders. We see the Holy Spirit and the sea of glass. We will use this "sea of glass" to identify the throne of God in later chapters. Around God's throne we see the four living creatures proclaiming God's Holiness. The twenty four elders lay their crowns before the throne and worship God.

In the right hand of God is a scroll with writing on both sides and sealed with seven seals. The only one worthy of opening the seals is our Lord and Savior Jesus Christ. Christ took the scroll from the right hand of God. The four creatures and 24 elders fell down before the Christ and sang a new song as the prayers of the saints are released.

"You are worthy to take the scroll
and to open its seals,
because you were slain,
and with your blood you purchased men for God

175

from every tribe and language and people and nation.
You have made them to be a kingdom and priests to serve
our God,
and they reign on the earth." (NIV)

Hundreds of million of angels surround the thrones and sing another song.

"Worthy is the Lamb, who was slain,
to receive power and wealth and wisdom and strength
and honor and glory and praise!" (NIV)

Every creature in heaven and on earth and under the earth and on the sea, and all that is in them are singing:

"To him who sits on the throne and to the Lamb
be praise and honor and glory and power,
for ever and ever!" (NIV)

So, here we see why Jesus Christ is the only one worthy to open the seals.

**Chapter 6** is where we see the seven seals judgments. These judgments are of particular importance to us because this is where we live now.

The first seal reveals a conqueror bent on conquest. As we look at the Babylonian, Medo-Persian, Greek, Roman and more recent conquest it is easy to see where one quarter of the world has been conquered at one time or another. It is doubtful that the world organizations will allow such massive invasions in the future.

The second seal reveals power to take peace from the earth and make man slay each other. I lived near Houston when it was the murder capital of the United States. Those killing were friends and families killing each other. There are still drug cartels fighting each other with little regard for who else is killed or injured. We still find evidence of mass

176

murders; but hopefully that will improve in the future. On the less destructive side we still have large conflicts between employer and employee. With a divorce rate hanging around 50% we see massive lack of peace in our most sacred unions. What happens to your peace when someone cuts you off in traffic? It is easy to see where peace has been removed from a quarter of people on earth today.

The third seal reveals problems in our economic system. As high tech, high paying, jobs are performed by the lowest bidder we see massive economic redistribution. It is harder and harder for the unemployed to find replacement occupations that pay the salary they have previously earned. That is contrasted by more and more millionaires being created each year. The lower earning employee must work more and more hours to purchase what they want. While the more affluent business owner or employee can afford the more luxurious products and residence. It is easy to imagine a quarter of the population of the earth being involved in some form of economic unbalance.

The fourth seal reveals Death, with Hades following close behind.

The last one hundred years has been the deadliest in the history of mankind. We are looking at deaths by sword (weapon), famine, plague (swine flue), and wild beast. As we continue to use wilderness for housing of one type or another we expose ourselves to animal encounters. We lose as many people to traffic and other accidents as we do to wars today. My understanding of Hades is that it is the underground abode of the dead in Greek mythology. There are more and larger grave yards everywhere. The incidents of gravesite contamination are more common each year and are likely to continue into the future. As more and more capacity is required at gravesites it is tempting to reuse very old gravesites for current needs.

The fifth seal reveals the souls of those who have been slain because of the word of God and the testimony they maintained. They are understandably anxious for judgment of those that killed them. They are told there are more to come and that they should be patient until the time is complete. Death because of your beliefs is not common in the United States but can be more of a threat in other parts of the World today. The white robes attest to their acceptance by God.

Mankind is about to crucify God's Earth as it did His Son. As the sixth seal is opened we see man's destruction of God's Earth. Every mountain and island was removed from its place. Long Island will no longer be there, it has been dumped into the ocean along with Bermuda and all other islands. The mountains of the World have been flattened. The earth is spinning out of orbit. It almost appears here that God is doing these things to the Earth; however, we will find later that mankind is doing these things to God's Earth. Something stopped the complete destruction of the Earth, was it our Lord and Savior rescuing us again? It sure is nice to have a loving God regardless of what we do.

What did we just see? We saw the destruction of God's Earth! But, we are about to go on as if nothing happened. This event has not occurred yet so we are within the time frame of the seal judgments. Something (God probably Jesus Christ) saved the Earth and set it back in proper orbit to allow human life to continue.

There is one other nagging event that confuses us. We know Satan had access to God during Job. The date of Job is unknown; however, the best guess is around the 2000 to 1800 B.C. time period. When Satan contended with Arch Angel Michael and was thrown out of Heaven and landed on Earth is not known. We know it was well before King Herod had all the male children less than two years old in Jerusalem killed.

**Chapter 7** finds God protecting His people from the judgments to come with the Trumpet judgments. After God's rescue of the Earth, after man's folly, there is no doubt that Jesus Christ exists and He is the Son of God. Is this where the Nation of Israel becomes a Christian Nation? Will their job be to bring the word of God to all the people of the Earth? Here God puts a seal on the forehead of all his servants. Do you think it will be long before Satan marks his followers? God marks 144,000 individuals from the twelve tribes of Israel as his servants.

John saw a great multitude that no one could count from every nation, tribe, people and language. They were standing before the throne of God and Christ. They were dressed in white robes signifying faithfulness to God through their years. Do you recognize yourself in this multitude? These are the Saints that have been gathered unto God. Are these the Saints that were harvested when the Earth was destroyed?

In **Chapter 8** Christ opens the seventh seal. As the seventh seal is opened the Trumpet judgments are started. Even before the first trumpet is sounded the prayers of the saints went up before God. The angel with the golden censer took fire from the altar and hurled it to Earth. The angel's action caused peals of thunder, rumbling, flashes of lighting and an earthquake.

As the first Trumpet is sounded there came hail and fire mixed with blood, and it was hurled down to Earth. A third of the Earth was burned up, a third of the trees were burned up, and all the green grass was burned up. Notice here that a third of things are burned up; whereas, in the seal judgments a quarter of things were destroyed. So the trumpet judgments are only about eight percent worse than the seal judgments as far as what part of the Earth is involved. However; the judgments are more severe.

When the second trumpet sounded a huge mountain was thrown into the sea. One third of the sea turned into blood. One third of the creatures of the sea died. One third of the ships were destroyed.

When the third trumpet sounded a great star blazing like a torch fell from the sky onto one third of the rivers and springs. The waters turned bitter and many people died from the bitter water.

When the fourth trumpet sounded one third of the sun, moon, and stars turned dark. A third of the day and night was without light.

An Eagle called out "Woe! Woe! Woe to the inhabitants of the earth, because of the trumpet blasts about to be sounded by the other three angels!" (NIV)

In **Chapter 9** when the fifth trumpet sounded a star fell from the sky to the Earth. The star was given the key to the Abyss. When the Abyss was opened smoke rose as if from a gigantic furnace. The sun and sky was darkened by the smoke. Locusts came out of the smoke and were given power like that of a scorpion. These locusts were told not to harm the grass or any plant or tree. They were told to harm only people who did not have the seal of God on their foreheads. They did not have the power to kill but only to torture those without the seal of God for five months. The agony they suffered was like that of a sting of a scorpion when it strikes people. During this five month period people without the seal of God will seek death but will not find death. They had as King over them the angel of the Abyss.

The four angels bound at the great river Euphrates in Chapter 7 were released to kill one third of mankind "The number of the mounted troops was two hundred million…" (NIV) That number of mounted troops suggests a much larger population and economy than exist on the Earth as we know it. There

180

must have been significant growth in the size of the Earth, population, and economy to support that number of mounted troops.

John gives a description of the vision he saw that was enough to give one nightmares. As bad as that was with the huge number of deaths the rest of mankind that was not killed did not repent. They continued to worship demons, and idols of gold, silver, bronze, stone and wood. They did not repent of their murders, magic arts, sexual immorality or thefts.

In **Chapter 10** another mighty angel comes down from heaven. This angel has a little scroll lying open in his hand. When this angel shouts the seven thunders spoke. John was instructed to not write what the seven thunders said.

This angel raised the right hand to heaven and swore "There will be no more delay!" (NIV) At the end of Chapter 9 we were told no one repented from their sins even with the severe torment that was inflicted on the people that did not have the seal of God on their forehead. God knows there will be no more conversion to followers of Christ; so it is time to end the reign of evil on the earth.

John was instructed to take the scroll from the angel and eat it. It tasted as sweet as honey when he ate it; but, it turned sour in his stomach. John was told he must Prophecy again about many people, nations, languages and kings.

In **Chapter 11** John was told to measure the temple of God and the altar, and to count the worshiper there. The outer court was not measured because it was open to the Gentiles for 42 months.

God's two witnesses were given power for 42 months. These two witnesses had a defense system to protect them from all who opposed them. They had power to control the Earth's water and could turn water to blood and strike the earth with every kind of plague as often as they want.

After the 42 months when they have completed their testimony the beast from the Abyss will attack them and kill them. Their bodies will lie in the street for 3 ½ days while the people of the Earth celebrate their departure. After 3 ½ days the breath of life from God will bring them back to life. When they stood on their feet the people were terrified. The two witnesses went up to heaven in a cloud while their enemies looked on.

The hour the witnesses departed a severe earthquake struck the earth and a tenth of the city collapsed. Seven thousand people were killed in the earthquake, and the survivors were terrified and gave glory to the God of heaven.

As the seventh trumpet is sounded a loud voice from heaven declared the world is now the kingdom of our Lord and his Christ. When God's temple was opened there came flashes of lighting, rumblings, and peals of thunder, an earthquake and great hailstorm. Things are about to change!

In **Chapter 12** we go back in time to the birth of Jesus. We see a cosmic version of the birth of Jesus, with the enormous red dragon waiting to devour Jesus the moment of birth. Mary gave birth to Jesus who will rule the nations with an iron scepter. God protected Mary from Satan and protected her for 1260 days, or 42 months or 3 ½ years. This is the time when Joseph took Mary and baby Jesus to Egypt where they would be safe from King Herod.

We see a war in heaven. Michael and his angels fought against the great red dragon and his angels. Satan lost and was hurled to earth with his angels. Was this battle over the decision to allow Jesus to offer his life for the salvation of the people on earth? We will never know; but, it makes sense. Satan was always in opposition to God's plans and this could have been the conflict that caused the separation of God and Satan. If there is any connection, then this is a clue to the time when Satan was forced to come to earth. That would be about the time of the birth of Christ. When

182

Satan was not successful with his plan to destroy Jesus he turned to the destruction of all Christians.

In **Chapter 13** we find Satan standing on the shore of the sea. He has been defeated by Michael and is looking to put together a team to return to the battle against God and all Christians. Satan called the beast from the sea. John's description of the beast made him seem like a selection of vicious animals. One head seemed to have had a fatal wound, but the wound had healed. Was this supposed to provide a counter for Christ's crucifixion and resurrection? The dragon gave the beast from the sea his power and his throne and great authority. The beast had great following among the people of the earth. The beast launched a propaganda campaign against God and all those in heaven. He made war against the saints and conquered them. The beast was given authority over every tribe, people, language and nation. All inhabitants of the earth, except the people whose names appear in the book of life, worshiped the beast.

Satan continued to build his team by calling forth a beast from the earth. This beast from the earth is given great authority and performs miraculous feats. He deceives the inhabitants of the earth and orders them to set up an image in honor of the beast that was wounded and yet lived. He gave breath to the image so it could speak. He caused all that refused to worship the image to be killed. He also caused all to receive a mark which is the mark of the beast. His umber is 666.

There are all kinds of speculation about the number 666. Some claim it is about the Roman Empire and its persecution of Christians. There is enough speculation about 666 to support just about any notion you may desire. However, the point is that this is not occurring during our time. Satan does not mark his people until after God has marked his own.

Satan has his command team complete and he is engaged in his attack on Christianity in any way he can. His greatest victories are when he can lead a Christian leader astray and cause them to sin in a way that discredits their church or organization.

In **Chapter 14** we flash back to the 144,000 redeemed from the twelve tribes of Israel. They have a new song that only they can sing. They stand on Mount Zion (Jerusalem) and have their heavenly father's name written on their foreheads. They are blameless.

John sees three angels, the first is bringing the message "Fear God and give him glory, because the hour of his judgment has come. Worship him who made the heavens, the earth, the sea and the springs of water." (NIV)

The second angel brings the message "Fallen! Fallen is Babylon the Great which made all the nations drink the maddening wine of her adulteries." (NIV)

The third angel brings another message. "If anyone worships the beast and his image and receives his mark on the forehead or on the hand, he too, will drink of the wine of God's fury, which has been poured full strength into the cup of his wrath. He will be tormented with burning sulfur in the presence of the holy angels and of the Lamb. And the smoke of their torment rises for ever and ever. There is no rest day or night for those who worship the beast and his image, or for anyone who receives the mark of his name." (NIV)

John was told to write "Blessed are the dead who die in the Lord from now on." "Yes." Says the Spirit, "they will rest from their labor, for their deeds will follow them." (NIV)

Here again we are told that our deeds, good and bad, will follow us into heaven or hell.

184

In the last part of Chapter 14 we see the two harvests of the Saints. Where you choose to place these two events determines what Revelation means to you. I choose to place one of the harvests at the end of Chapter 6. After God rescues the earth the first harvest comes. When God intercedes and corrects man's folly by restoring Earth to its proper orbit, there can be no doubt that Jesus Christ exists and He is the Son of God. That knowledge causes the nation of Israel to become a Christian nation and the 144,000 take the word of God to the nations of the world. When the work of the 144,000 is done, there is no more conversion to Christianity, and then it is time to complete God's war on sin and evil. I place the second harvest of Saints at the time when the work of the 144,000 is complete. How do you read it? Do you have a different belief? Please let me hear how you feel about these two passages (Revelation 14:14-16 and Revelation 14:17-20)

In **Chapter 15** we are introduced to the song of Moses.

"Great and marvelous are your deeds,
Lord God Almighty.
Just and true are your ways,
King of the ages.
Who will not hear you, O Lord,
and bring glory to your name?
For you alone are holy.
All nations will come and worship before you,
for your righteous acts have been revealed." (NIV)

We are introduced to the seven angels that will bring the seven bowl judgments.

**Chapter 16** completes the bowl judgments; God's justice is swift and complete. Remember these are total judgments; no part of the earth will be spared.

The first bowl causes ugly and painful sores to break out on the people who have the mark of the beast and worship his image.

The second bowl causes the sea to turn to blood and every living thing in the sea dies.

The third bowl causes all the springs of water to become blood.

The fourth bowl causes the sun to scorch people with fire; but, the people refused to repent and glorify God.

The fifth bowl caused the kingdom of the beast to be plunged into darkness; but, they refused to repent of what they had done.

The sixth bowl caused the great river Euphrates to dry up and Satan's forces prepare for battle.

The seventh bowl announced "It is done." There came flashes of lightning, rumblings, peals of thunder and a sever earthquake. Every island fled away and the mountains could not be found. From the sky huge hailstones of about 100 pounds fell upon men. And they cursed God because the plague was so terrible.

Even at this extreme there were no conversions to Christ. I am sure glad we will not be exposed to these extremes.

In **Chapter 17** we find the great prostitute. Her world is dominated by materialism. On her forehead are the words:

MYSTERY
BABYLON THE GREAT
THE MOTHER OF PROSTITUTES
AND OF THE ABOMINATIONS OF THE EARTH (NIV)

She is totally consumed in the pursuit of pleasure and consumption. There is no place for compassion, respect or gratitude within her being. The woman's gaudy dress and accessories further confirm her total indulgence in material things. Once the character of the prostitute is established the nature of evil is revealed.

Rome was built on seven hills and this is where the prostitute sits.

There is a great history lesson about the rise and fall of the Roman Empire in verses 9 through 14. If you are so inclined it is an interesting study but has little to do with the story of Revelation.

In **Chapter 18** we see the fall of Babylon. The fall of Babylon is announced and a voice from heaven calls God's people out of her. The Kings that shared her materialism see Babylon going up in smoke. They stand far off and mourn her destruction. The merchants of the earth mourn her because they have no one to buy their cargoes. The transportation systems are also stressed because of the loss of trade.

While those in Chapter 18 mourn the fall of Babylon, God's people rejoice in **Chapter 19** because of the fall of Babylon. We go from the anguish of the failure of the world economic system to the wedding of the Jesus Christ to his church.

Jesus Christ appears on a white horse and is called Faithful and True. His eyes are like blazing fire as He cuts through all deception, lies and half truths. His judgments are just and true. Jesus is dressed in a robe dipped in blood and his name is Word of God. On His robe and thigh He has the name written:

# KING OF KINGS AND LORD OF LORDS

An angel called to all birds to come eat the flesh of kings, generals, and mighty men, of horses and their riders, and the flesh of all people, free and slave, small and great. The final battle is about to begin.

The beast and kings of the earth gather their armies and prepare for battle. But the beast and the false prophet was captured and thrown into the lake of burning sulfur. The rest of them were killed by the sword that came out of the mouth of the rider on the horse. All the birds gorged themselves on their flesh.

In **Chapter 20** we learn about the 1000 year confinement of Satan. An angel came down from heaven with a great chain and bound Satan. The angel threw Satan in the Abyss and locked and sealed it over him. Satan can no longer deceive the nations until the 1000 years is over. This will be a period of 1000 years of peace and prosperity as Jesus Christ rules all the nations of the earth. After the 1000 years is up, Satan will be released for a short time. How can you tell a true believer from one that is only pretending to believe? Would it be better to test?

After the thousand years is over Satan is released and goes out to the nations of the world to prepare for battle with God's people. Satan deceives the nations to bring them to battle. The numbers brought to battle are like the sand on the seashore. They gather and surround the camp of God's people. Fire comes down from heaven and devours them. Turns out it was God's battle not man's battle. Satan was thrown into the lake of burning sulfur. Where Satan, the beast, and false profit will be tormented day and night for ever and ever.

John saw a great white throne with him who was seated on it. John saw the dead, great and small, standing before the

188

throne. The books were opened. The dead were judged according to what they had done as recorded in the books. Death and Hades were thrown into the lake of burning sulfur. If anyone's name was not found written in the book of life, he was thrown into the lake of fire.

John here is black and white, there is no other option. However; the question remains where are the people for the nations that the Saints will rule over with Christ? Are there people in the book of life that cannot be included in the New Jerusalem? Could these be people that confessed their belief in Christ but did not live their lives according to the way Christians should behave? Or is there an option that will allow people to choose to live in the New Jerusalem or in the New Earth? I'll leave that for you to ponder.

In **Chapter 21** John saw the new heaven and new earth. The first heaven and earth had passed away and there was no longer any sea. John saw the Holy City, the New Jerusalem, coming down from heaven. A loud voice from the throne proclaimed that God will reside with mankind and that there will be no more tears, death, mourning, or pain for the old things have passed away.

Another proclamation from the throne declared "I am making everything new!" Looks like the handyman will no longer be needed if everything is always new.

Still another announcement he who overcomes will inherit all this, and I will be his God and he will be my son.

The cowardly, the nonbeliever, the vile, the murderers, the sexually immoral, and those who practice magic arts, the idolaters and all liars will be placed in the lake of burning sulfur.

John saw the New Jerusalem and it shone with the glory of God and its brilliance was like that of a very precious jewel.

The great high wall surrounding it had twelve gates three on each side. Each gate had the name of one of the twelve tribes of Israel written on it. The wall had twelve foundations, one for each of the twelve apostles.

The width of the wall was 144 Cubits (216 feet to 252 feet thick). We are not told how high the great high wall is, only how thick. However, entry into the New Jerusalem is through one of the 12 gates so it must be a pretty high wall to allow all traffic to and from all the nations of the New Earth.

The Holy City was a cube of 12,000 stadia on each dimension. If we use the Roman measure the 12,000 stadia would be 1379 miles cube. If you tried to put that size of a city on our earth it would sink, throw the earth out of balance, and probably send it whirling out into space. So, this earth that receives the New Jerusalem is a much larger place than the earth we know today. With God being with us we do not need the universe. Did God use all the material in the universe to create the New Earth and New Jerusalem? The New Jerusalem was the same shape as in the inner sanctuary in the Old Testament.

John did not see a temple in the city. God Almighty and the Lamb is its temple. There is no need for the sun or moon for the glory of God gives it light and the Lamb is its lamp. There is no night. Your new home is luxurious beyond your wildest imagination. Only those whose names are written in the Lamb's book of life will enter the New Jerusalem.

In **Chapter 22** we see the river where the waters of life flow from the throne of God and the Lamb. The river flows down the Great Street of the city with the tree of life on each side of the river. The tree of life bears twelve forms of fruit and its leaves are used to heal the nations. There will no longer be any curse, no more weeds! No more weeds would put the joy back into gardening. You can forget about power failures

190

here because Lord God provides the light, there will be no more night.

Jesus told John "Behold, I am coming soon! My reward is with me, and I will give to everyone according to what he has done..." (NIV) Again it is clearly stated that your reward will be according to what you have done. Go now and build your eternal reward.

Revelation closes with Jesus saying "Yes, I am coming soon." (NIV)

May the grace of the Lord Jesus be with God's People always! Amen

Thank you for reading my book;
if you like it tell your friends.
If you did not like it please tell me at
scotty80@juno.com


If you have any questions, suggestions,
corrections, comments, criticisms
or referrals please send me an email at
scotty80@juno.com.